TACKLING TOUGH ISSUES

Is It Really So? — *The Village Reporter*

Is It Really So? is the title of a weekly newspaper column written by Jerry Bergman for *The Village Reporter* of Montpelier, Ohio. Bergman had been writing a similar column for *The Bryan Times* of Bryan, Ohio, for over a decade until the paper's editor disagreed with several of Bergman's Christian articles and discontinued the column. Bergman then took copies of several of his past articles to *The Village Reporter* editor for review. The *Reporter* decided to publish the weekly, one-thousand-word column, now going on three years.

One difference between *The Village Reporter* and *The Bryan Times* was that *The Bryan Times* leans politically left and is not always supportive of the Christian worldview. Bergman's column has covered a wide variety of topics of general interest, including Donald Trump, Jews, World War II, eugenics, global warming, Hamas War, Christianity, the transgenderism controversy, the Scopes trial, racism, Christmas, the Nazi Holocaust, the problems of mothers and fathers, and other topics.

Most of the articles respond to current events or Bergman's experiences that he concludes are of interest to general readers. He has worked in a large state prison, for the courts as a researcher, and at Arlington Psychological Associates Clinic as a licensed therapist. The column, published since 2022 in *The Village Reporter*, was titled "Is It Really So?"—a title selected by the editor.

The first edition of *Tackling Tough Issues* was a small printing of a compilation of forty-nine articles published in 2024 from *The Village Reporter* column. This second edition includes slight editing to improve readability and corrections of a few minor errors. The second edition was designed to be a permanent record of the 2023 column. The dates associated with the article titles reflect the publication dates of the print edition of *The Village Reporter* and not the dates of the articles posted online.

Tackling Tough Issues

CURRENT TOPICS IN *THE VILLAGE REPORTER*, MONTPELIER, OHIO

Second Edition

Jerry Bergman

Creation Summit

LINDHURST, IL

Published by
Creation Summit, Lindhurst, Illinois

First edition published 2024. Second edition 2025.

Printed in the United States of America

Distributed by
Amazon.com

Because of the dynamic nature of the internet, any web addresses or links contained in this book may have changed since publication and may no longer be valid.

Views expressed in this work are solely those of the author and do not necessarily reflect the views of the publisher, and the publisher hereby disclaims any responsibility for them.

Bergman, Jerry, 1946–
    Tackling tough issues. Second Edition

ISBN: 979-8-9950778-0-0 (soft cover)

A Brief Word to the Reader

Got a minute? Then those sixty seconds would be best invested in reading one of the engaging *Village Reporter* vignettes authored by Dr. Jerry R. Bergman. Possessing nine academic degrees, Dr. Bergman is, nevertheless, able to connect with the average layperson (and to the above-average citizen like yourself) with a very down-to-earth, winsome style.

Don't get me wrong! The myriads of topics addressed in this captivating compendium will serve to enlighten, thrill, challenge, and/or delight you. You will find your mind stimulated, your emotions stirred, your memory reminiscing, and maybe even yourself motivated to act, get involved with a cause, and/or make a positive difference in this troubled, needy world.

Who better to spend a minute (*or longer*) with than a fascinating individual who is a master of information quite capable of clearly and concisely communicating? So sit back and redeem those sixty (*or more*) seconds with a seasoned professor, a voracious reader, and a prolific author who is known for being a writer of the readable and a researcher of the relevant. Enjoy!

—David V. Bassett, MS

Endorsement

Drawing upon his extensive research and writings, Dr. Bergman in this work deals with a wide array of current issues, as well as personal experiences, from a creationist and Biblical understanding.

Many of the entries were triggered by special days of the calendar year, such Martin Luther King Jr. Day, Mother's Day, Father's Day, and Christmas. Other topics were chosen as they continue to be of great concern for our culture's future, including the problem of gender dysphoria, affirmative action policies, the COVID vaccine questions, climate alarmists, and illegal immigration. These issues receive almost continuous coverage in our media, and Dr. Bergman provides a reasoned, scientifically sound Biblical approach to each.

In this multivaried work, Dr. Bergman also deals with topics specific to the creation/evolution debate, such as the Scopes Trial, the Galileo incident, the well-designed human eye, the Darwinist path to eugenics and the holocaust, and the censorship of Darwin doubters in academia, among other topics.

Finally, Dr. Bergman shares from his own life experience, both professionally and on a personal level. These experiences range from correspondence with a death row inmate to luncheons with the president of the nation of Fiji, from memorials to his parents, and a lost friend, to praise for his wife. This work is not only highly informative but also gives the reader a glimpse into the person of Dr. Jerry Bergman. I highly recommend it.

—Kirk Toth, BS (biology)

Contents

Introduction

I have now completed a weekly column consisting of an average of 750 words for an entire year. I originally expected to do one column a month, but the feedback was so positive, and there is now so much to write about, that I did fifty-one columns. The problem was each week I had to decide, of the many possible topics that interest me, which one do I write about? In an eventful week I would often do two columns and only send one in. I now have about thirty columns ready to go in case we have a slow news week. I had been doing a *The Bryan Times* (this is the local Bryan, Ohio paper) column once a month for close to thirty years but was told I was too controversial, and they would no longer publish my columns.

Don't I wish some of my articles were even slightly controversial! Out of the fifty-one columns I did for *The Village Reporter* only one engendered a letter of complaint: only one! In response to the concern, I did another column to respond to the issues raised by the writer. Otherwise, the most common feedback by far was, "I really enjoyed reading your newest column. It was excellent." The fact that my *Bryan Times* articles were censored, allowed me to join a large collection of distinguished authors who can claim the moniker "censored." The circulation of *The Village Reporter* covers two Ohio counties, Williams and Fulton counties, which are home to twenty-eight cities with a combined readership of 2,400 persons per week.

As a professor for over forty years, I have learned student dialogue is critical to effective learning. I am not the kind of professor that drones on, putting students to sleep. Students learn by interacting with ideas and information. To elicit student dialogue requires thought-provoking course content. Many columns are the "*Reader's Digest*" of one of my books, thus the reader can get the gist of the information in a three-hundred-page book in a few minutes. Most of the columns are as relevant today as they were when they were first published. They were reproduced here exactly as they were first published, save a few typos which were corrected and some clarification such as the findings of the new James Webb telescope. If you are like me, I enjoy rereading articles that I found useful the first time that I read them. I have forty-five four-drawer file cabinets packed with information from various print sources that I would like to use in the future. I also publish four articles a month, now totaling 301 articles, mostly on science, apologetics, and Christianity on my website: crev.info.

People ask where I get my ideas to write about. Since I was in high school, I have read about a book a week. Now I cannot do that because I have writing commitments which are a priority. I do watch each evening an hour-long documentary on science, nature, history, World War II, the Civil Rights Movement, or a biography. This helps me relax before I go to bed. My watching amounts to 365 hours a year; much more time in total than I spent in a college classroom when I was a full-time student. I buy most of my documentaries at Half-Price Books or on eBay, as they can be very expensive if purchased new. Most stores that sell used videos, such as Goodwill, rarely have documentaries, and, with few exceptions, I rarely watch movies.

The Village Reporter
115 Broad St, Montpelier, OH 43543

Forrest R. Church, Publisher

The paper serves Williams County, population thirty-seven thousand and Fulton County, population forty-two thousand.

When *The Bryan Times* censored me after thirty-five years of publishing with them, I went to *The Village Reporter* and gave them copies of the censored columns. They liked them and offered me an opportunity to do a column for them. The plan was once a month as I did for *The Bryan Times*, but the feedback was so positive that I ended up doing a weekly column for them. The circulation of *The Village Reporter*, I was told, after I began my column for them, increased.

January 4, 2023. We Believe God Has Had a Special Role for America

We today hear an almost constant stream of America bashing. Watching the news, we hear that America is a systemically racist and sexist society dominated by racist white supremacists, both when it was founded and still today. As a college student studying history, I traveled to Europe in 1966 to learn history firsthand. In my three weeks there, my assignment was to study not only historic sites, such as the Colosseum in Rome, but the contemporary culture. This entailed visiting a wide variety of retail stores. In an office supply store, I noted that most items were not only made in the United States but were *invented* here. Examples included Scotch tape, including Post-it® notes (invented in 1925 by Richard Drew), Swingline staplers (invented in 1866 by George McGill), and the typewriter (invented in 1868 by Christopher Sholes).

Most people are aware of the major American inventions that forever changed the world, including the airplane, telegraph, telephone, cell phone (the first mobile phone in 1973 weighed nearly four-and-a-half pounds), television, the transistor, robotics, motion pictures, the phonograph, and most portable power tools (such as Skil and Black & Decker). Visiting an appliance store, I soon added most modern kitchen appliances to my list of American inventions. This included the electric stove, microwave oven (invented in 1945), refrigerator, washing machine, clothes dryer, dishwasher, and the electric iron.

America has continued to lead the world since then with photocopiers (Xerox in 1959) and lasers (developed in 1960) used for surgery, welding, DVD players, and fiber optics. Now light-emitting diodes (LEDs, 1962) light up the world, replacing the old inferior incandescent street lights as well as home and office lights. Other examples include Global Positioning Satellites (GPS) and chemotherapy (which produced major declines in cancer-mortality rates). Even magnetic resonance imaging (MRI), the most important new diagnostic tool of the last century, was invented by the American medical doctor, Raymond Damadian in New York. Video games were also invented here, which led to the development of high-tech machines to train airline pilots and other skilled workers. And the list goes on: practical personal computers (Apple 1, released in 1975), the internet (1983), and email (1971).

The American movie industry has dominated the world for the last century. As of 2017, it had produced the second-largest number of films of any single country after China, with more than seven hundred English-language films released annually. In sales, the United States ranks among the world's largest book publishers, including Harper Collins, Houghton Mifflin, Harcourt, McGraw-Hill, Scholastic, Simon & Schuster, and Wiley. Paper and gunpowder were invented in China over a thousand years ago, and the metal movable-type printing press in Europe, along with innovations in type casting was invented in Germany in 1450, but I could not find a single major invention invented *outside* of America during the last two centuries! The major reason for America's overwhelming success is that, as a capitalist country, we have the freedom to try and fail. And if we succeed, we have the potential to become very rich, as many Americans have. It is no exaggeration to note that America has contributed more to the material progress of the world in the past century than the entire world has during the forty previous centuries. No other country has the freedom, money, mineral resources, sales market size, and encouragement required to develop one's full creative potential than does America. God has, indeed, richly blessed America, and America has, in turn, blessed the entire world. May His blessings (*and mercy*) continue still.

January 11, 2023. The US Supreme Court: Highly Respected … But Not Perfect!

Most US Supreme Court decisions, even the controversial ones, eventually become settled law. A decade later, most people wonder, "How could the Court have ruled any other way?" American Supreme Court rulings often have ramifications throughout the world. The laws of other nations, especially Western nations, are heavily influenced by our Court's decisions, and they often cite our Court's rulings to defend their own rulings.

The Supreme Court is the most powerful institution in America. Yet it is fallible, as are all human institutions. The total number of rulings since the Court was established in 1790 runs into the thousands. Although 98 percent still stand, even today, a few rulings were so bad that they were overturned by the Supreme Court itself in later years. Actually, 232 of its own case rulings have been reversed by a subsequent US Supreme Court since 1810.

Among the worst Supreme Court decisions was *Dred Scott v. Sandford*, 60 US 393 (1857). Sadly, the Court, in a 7-to-2 decision, supported the prevailing scientific thought of that time by asserting that "Negroes" were an inferior "race," less-evolved than the Caucasian "race." Specifically, the Court held that "Black" people were not intended to be included as citizens under the Constitution. Therefore, they could claim none of the rights and privileges secured to citizens of the United States. The Court ruled that "Negroes" were, for more than a century, "regarded as beings of an inferior order and altogether unfit to associate with the white race, either in social or political relations; and so far inferior that they had no rights which the white man was bound to respect."

Dred Scott was a slave owned by an army physician who had taken him from Missouri, a slave-holding state, into Illinois, where slavery was illegal. When his owner brought him back to Missouri, he [Scott] claimed that, because he had been taken into a "free" US territory, he was legally no longer a slave. In 1846, Scott and his wife, aided by antislavery lawyers, sued for their freedom and eventually lost in the Supreme Court. This ruling was the law of the land for the next half century.

Laws in the United States called "Jim Crow" statutes were based on the racial inferiority belief. In 1896, Homer A. Plessy challenged racist laws by deliberately violating Louisiana's *Separate Car Act of 1890,* also known as *The Withdraw Car Act* (Act 111). The 1890 Act required "equal, but separate" train car accommodations for White and non-White passengers based on the Darwinian superior-inferior race belief. Plessy was an octoroon, a person seven-eighths "White" and a mere one-eighth "Black," who physically appeared 100 percent Caucasian. It was for this reason that he was thought to be an excellent candidate to challenge the existing racist law. Plessy's attorney, Albion W. Tourgée, correctly argued that the 1890 Separate Car Act was based on the wrong belief in the inferiority of African Americans compared to the superiority of "Whites."

The Supreme Court in *Plessy v. Ferguson*, 163 US 537, ruled, "If one race be inferior to the other socially, the Constitution of the United States cannot put them upon the same plane" (*Plessy v. Ferguson*, 544, 552)." It took almost another half-century for the Supreme Court to overturn *Plessy v. Ferguson*, specifically in the *Brown, et al. v. Board of Education of Topeka, et al.* (347 US 483 (1954)). The Supreme Court in the Brown case ruled, "Separate educational facilities are inherently unequal. Therefore, we hold that [the complainant was] deprived of the equal protection of the laws guaranteed by the Fourteenth Amendment (Brown 1954, 488, 495)." The Brown ruling was a major step in overturning the belief in the evolutionary inferiority of certain "races."

In the twentieth century, a movement called Darwinian eugenics was supported by many scientists and medical doctors. They believed that inferior persons, both Black and White, should be sterilized to prevent them from producing more inferior persons like themselves. The movement faced opposition from Black and White churches and persons who believed that all men were created in the image of God, thus in the eyes of God were equal.

To silence the opposition, the eugenicists brought a case all the way to the Supreme Court. The Court sided with the eugenicists, ruling that an uneducated white girl, Carrie Buck, could be sterilized against her will. The eugenics lobby used this case to open the door to massive Darwinian eugenic sterilizations for the thousands of people they deemed unfit to reproduce due to what the Darwin eugenics supporters judged as their evolutionary and mental inferiority. The highly respected Supreme Court justice, Oliver Wendell Holmes, sanctioned state-enforced sterilization of so-called inferior persons based on Darwinian eugenics, claiming that

> heredity plays an important part in the transmission of insanity, imbecility. ...It is better for all the world, if instead of waiting to execute degenerate offspring for crime, or to let them starve for their imbecility, society can prevent those who are manifestly unfit from continuing their kind. The principle that sustains compulsory vaccination is broad enough to cover cutting the fallopian tubes. Three generations of imbeciles are enough (*Buck v. Bell* 1927, 206–207).

Actually, Carrie ended up in an institution only because, as a pregnant young girl without a family member willing to take her in, it was the best choice for her then. Furthermore, in contrast to the judge's claim, Carrie, a life-long avid reader, lived into her seventies. And those who found themselves against her in a bridge game had no reason whatsoever to believe that she was "feeble-minded" or anything close.

Nonetheless, this 8-to-1 Supreme Court decision opened the eugenic floodgates, soon resulting in over sixty-four thousand eugenic sterilizations in America. This ruling also influenced the Nazis to copy the American law, forcibly sterilizing 375 thousand putatively "inferior" Germans. At the Nuremberg War Crime trials, the Nazis who carried out forced eugenic sterilizations in Germany cited the *Buck v. Bell* case as their motivation and, likewise, as their defense in the Nuremberg trials.

In *Minersville Schools v. Gobitis* (310 US 586 (1940)), the Supreme Court ruled that the state could force students to salute the US flag and recite the Pledge of Allegiance against their will. The extent of the enforcement even included being expelled from school and removal from their parents' home. The Court ruled:

> Two youths, now fifteen and sixteen years of age, are by the judgment of this Court held liable to expulsion from the public schools and to denial of all publicly supported educational privileges because of their refusal to yield to the compulsion of a law which commands their participation in a school ceremony (Minersville Schools 1940, 601).

The decision affected many religious sects, including the Mennonites, Amish, Children of Israel, Church of God, and Jehovah's Witnesses. To be consistent, several churches held that if it was wrong to force Germans to salute Hitler's swastika flag, it should also be wrong to force Americans to salute their flag.

This decision led eminent jurist Archibald Cox to write that, in America—a country claiming to be a champion of religious freedom—"The principal victims of religious persecution in the United States in the twentieth century were the Jehovah's Witnesses." The outrage, riots, beatings, and killings that objectors endured were so horrific after the *Gobitis* decision that it was overturned only three years later by *West Virginia State Board of Education v. Barnette*, 319 US 624 (1943). The decision held that the First Amendment Free Speech Clause protects students from being forced, under pain of severe punishment, to salute any flag or say any Pledge. With this ruling the persecution of the objector sects was greatly reduced and, in most cases, ended. This decision holds today and protects a variety of minority sects. We can be very thankful that the courts finally got it right. Biology has confirmed that there are no races, only the one race, the human race.

January 18, 2023. Why We Celebrate Martin Luther King Jr. Day

Now that Martin Luther King Jr. Day is here, some people have asked why we celebrate it. One reason is he is a good role model for young people today. Another reason is he changed America forever. I never met him, but a distant cousin of mine with the same name as mine, Dr. Gerald Bergman (he went by Walter), worked with him on the Freedom Ride. In the training for the Freedom Ride, the riders had to learn to take verbal and physical abuse to conform to Dr. King's nonviolence position. One well-built Black man did not deal will with the mocking verbal abuse. So, Dr. King sent him home.

As a Baptist minister, he consistently applied the Scriptures to his life, even to his civil rights philosophy. He recognized, correctly, that the scriptural teaching is clear, including to love your enemies and to turn the other cheek, meaning to refrain from retaliating when attacked or insulted. It's easy to love those who love you, but very difficult to love those who verbally abuse you. King correctly recognized that most people sympathized, not with bullies, but with persons who were unjustly abused.

In 1960, the Supreme Court integrated all interstate buses and bus stations. The Congress of Racial Equality (CORE) decided to test the Court's decision by sending an interracial team of civil rights workers called the Freedom Riders into the Deep South to use the newly integrated facilities. On Saturday night, May 13, 1961, the Freedom Rider group had dinner with Martin Luther King Jr. The next day two buses left, a Greyhound and a Trailways, to test the law by integrating the buses and the restaurants on the trip.

In Anniston, Alabama, the Trailways bus driver told the seven Black and three White Freedom Riders, that "Blacks, get to the back of the bus. White people, up front." None moved, and no one spoke. Then, the bus doors burst open and eight White men pushed their way past the driver. After pulling iron bars and chains from paper bags, the eight yanked the Blacks from their seats and pushed them to the back of the bus.

Walter Bergman, then sixty-one, was pushed to the floor and kicked repeatedly in the head. Behind them, Bergman's wife, Frances, fifty-eight, heard the sound of human flesh being brutally beaten for the first time in her life. Frances pleaded with the men to stop. She said later, "I had never before experienced the feeling of people all around hating me so. …I kept thinking, 'How could these things be happening in 1961?'" Soon after this Walter had a stroke and spent the rest of his life paralyzed in a wheelchair. Such was the cost of fighting for civil rights in the 1960s. This example was repeated thousands of times in the forty-year-long Civil Rights Movement from 1960 to the year 2000 when most of their goals were fulfilled.

Where did they get the strength to go through this? Why did Dr. King feel so strongly about this struggle which is still going on today? As a Christian he believed we are all children of Adam and Eve, our first parents. Thus, Blacks and Whites are all brothers. Dr. King was sharply critical of the misuse of science to promote racial discrimination, and he also spoke forcefully against the belief that humans are the products of a blind material process as evolution teaches. In a collection of sermons titled *Strength to Love*, King condemned modern scientific materialism, writing:

> To believe that human personality is the result of the fortuitous interplay of atoms and electrons is as absurd as to believe that a monkey, by hitting typewriter keys at random, will eventually produce a Shakespearean play. Sheer magic! It is much more sensible to say with Sir James Jeans, the physicist, that "the universe seems to be nearer to a great thought than to a great machine," or with Arthur Balfour, the philosopher, that "we now know too much about matter to be materialists." Materialism is a weak flame that is blown out by the breath of mature thinking. This universe is not a tragic expression of meaningless chaos but a marvelous display of orderly cosmos.

He bemoaned the results of "when Darwin's *Origin of Species* replaced belief in Creation by the theory of evolution." King also was a fierce critic of scientism, the claim that modern science is the only route to truth and we must rely on science to save society. King mockingly wrote that modern man had rewritten the Twenty-Third Psalm as:

> Science is my shepherd; I shall not want. It maketh me to lie down in green pastures: It leadeth me beside the still waters. It restoreth my soul…. I will fear no evil: for science is with me; Its rod and its staff they comfort me. Then Came the Big Bang Explosion [from which everything else evolved].

King was not antiscience, acknowledging, "The achievements of science have been marvelous, tangible, and concrete." But he warned, "The means by which we live have outdistanced the ends for which we live. Our scientific power has outrun our spiritual power."

King observed that those who formerly turned to God to find solutions for their problems now turned to science and technology, convinced that they now possessed the instruments required to usher in a new society without God. He believed that Darwinian theory, in particular, had been used to promote utopian thinking, writing: "Herbert Spencer skillfully molded the Darwinian theory of evolution into the heady idea of automatic progress. Men became convinced that there is a sociological law of progress that is as valid as the physical law of gravitation." But, he added, things didn't work out quite the way some had hoped:

> Then came the explosion of this myth. It climaxed in the horrors of Nagasaki and Hiroshima and in the fierce fury of fifty-megaton bombs. Now we have come to see that science can give us only physical power, which, if not controlled by spiritual power, will lead inevitably to cosmic doom.

These wise words were spoken by a man whose birthday is now a federal holiday, Martin Luther King Jr. Day, observed on the third Monday of January each year.

January 25, 2023. Differences Between Men and Women

After I earned my license, I began working for Arlington Psychological Associates. Most of my clients were women, and one of the main problems they dealt with was husbands or boyfriends. It soon became apparent that their problem was men did not understand the many differences between the sexes. This generalization does not apply to most couples but was a problem common to women seeking help at our psychological clinic. One memorable example was a couple in marriage counseling. One of her complaints was he rarely told her he loved her. His response was "I told you I loved you when we married, and if it changes, I will let you know."

To earn a PhD degree requires original research, ideally a project that will produce results. In medical school a few students pursued a project that did not produce meaningful results, so had to start over on another experiment. Students are normally allowed five years to complete the research. Some never earn their degree because they fail to produce valid research results. One easy quick project that most always produces good results is to compare males and women using functional magnetic resonance brain imaging (fMRI). This technique determines the specific brain location where a certain function, such as speech or memory, occurs. Comparisons have consistently documented differences between the sexes. In researching how colors are related to emotions, fMRI registers clear brain differences between males and females. The student then writes up the results and is awarded her PhD.

For years, only males were tested to determine proper drug dosage. It was then learned that a much higher rate of women taking Ambien were too sleepy to drive safely in the morning. Research found that women metabolized the drug differently than males. Consequently, women got twice the proper dose, which produced a rash of traffic accidents. A major reason for the difference was due to male and female hormone differences. Another example is women have lower levels of alcohol dehydrogenase in their stomach. This is the enzyme that breaks down ethanol. Thus, alcohol has a stronger, earlier effect in women than men. Now all new drugs must be evaluated on both sexes to determine the proper dosage.

Except for enucleated cells, every healthy normal human body cell, ignoring aneuploidy, is either male (XY) or female (XX). Given fifty trillion cells in the healthy human body, and forty-six chromosomes, the average human has 2,300,000,000,000,000 chromosomal differences compared to the opposite sex. Furthermore, the male Y chromosome contains fifty-five genes, and the X chromosome as many as 1,400 genes, or over twenty-five times as many genes. These 1,400 genes produce many of the major genetic differences existing between the sexes.

After a fertilized egg (zygote) is formed, thousands of other genetic differences are created by imprinting. Imprinting is where certain genes are switched off in males and other genes are switched off in females. Research on 118 fetuses, between twenty-six and forty weeks old found significant differences between males and females in seven of sixteen functional connectivity networks. These observations confirm the fact that sexual dimorphism emerges very early during human gestation.

A recent study of 1,065 brains found differences between male and female brains were so profound that scientists successfully predicted a dissected brain belonged to a man or woman with 93 percent accuracy. Another evaluation of 949 brain scans found a stark difference in the architecture of the brain that documents why men excel at certain tasks and women at others. Men are better at learning and performing a single task (cycling or navigating); women were better at multitasking. Men are better on spatial processing and sensory motor speed. Women are better than men on tasks related to attention, word, and facial memory. This research is evidence that male and female brains complement each other in life, work, and raising children.

Other research determined that women's pupils are 9 percent larger than men's, which gives rise to the saying that mothers and female teachers have "eyes in the back of their heads." Men have fewer rod visual cells and women have better color perception. One out of twelve men are color blind, compared to only one in every two hundred women. Men have greater sensitivity for fine detail and rapidly moving objects due to their 25 percent higher androgen receptors than females. Women have much better high-frequency hearing and listen by using both sides of their brain, whereas men are more likely to listen with only one side. Women have a better sense of smell because female brains have 50 percent more olfactory neurons. Women also have a better sense of taste due to more neurons in their brain taste center.

One of the results due to genetic difference is that females tend to choose careers that produce more personal rewards, even if the pay is less. Males tend to choose better-paying careers over those they prefer because income is often, for them, a major career consideration. Women as a whole make better neurosurgeons due to their superior fine-muscle coordination. Men make better diesel mechanics due to their superior gross-muscle coordination. Women lean toward careers focusing on people, such as teaching and healthcare. Males tend to work with things and are oriented to the engineering, manufacturing, and agricultural professions.

Conversely, some women make better diesel mechanics than most men. Some men, like Dr. Ben Carson, make better neurosurgeons than most women. In spite of spending millions to motivate women to earn degrees in welding and men in early child care, these efforts have failed. Studies have consistently found that differences in how men and women organize their verbal and visual-spatial abilities exist in every society. Males and females display major biological differences from zygote to death. This confirms the biblical teaching that God created human males and females for different, but compatible, roles. Marriage success required males and females to understand and accommodate for these differences.

February 8, 2023. A Murderer Murdered

In 1986 I received a call from the state of Texas asking me if I could provide insight in a murder case. After the details of the case were described, I felt I could be helpful. My experience includes working in the field of corrections and publishing widely in corrections. From my experience consulting in over a hundred court cases, including a number of murder and rape cases, the Texas murder case sent to me appeared a clear-cut case. The more I learned about it, though, the more I realized it was a very unusual case. The state claimed in 1985, after James Allridge III robbed a store of $300, he realized the clerk could recognize him because they had taken a management training course together. Goaded on by his older brother, he shot twenty-one-year-old Brian Clendennen who was then working in a Fort Worth, Texas, convenience store. Brian died the next day.

James was convicted, and his case was on appeal when I received the call from Texas. His court-appointed attorney sent me the complex record of the investigation and the two-thousand-page trial transcript. I also have now corresponded extensively with James. He had no previous criminal record, was an excellent student, but fell under the control and demands of an older, violent paranoid schizophrenic brother. James maintained a 4.0 GPA in the college courses he pursued while on death row and his top-notch art-work was exhibited in several locations including colleges. I also have a shoe box full of his letters proving art was not his only talent.

After I had prepared to testify in James's re-trial, his attorney was appointed a judge, and James's case was assigned to another attorney who had to start over. I informed his new attorney the details of the case, which I had to repeat each time James was appointed a new attorney for similar reasons. As is his right, he never got his day in court beyond the first trial, nor did I have a chance to present my exculpatory findings. Nor did the witnesses who were to testify at his re-trial.

The case received a lot of publicity. Academy Award-winning actress Susan Sarandon even made a special trip to death row to visit Allridge. After her two-hour visit with him she released this written statement:

> My heart and prayers go out to the Clendennen family. They have suffered a terrible loss, one that I would not presume to know. I hope they have found a way towards healing from the senseless murder of Brian. My friendship with James Allridge in no way diminishes my feelings of sympathy for the Clendennen family. It merely reflects the fact that James Allridge is a human being and he is much more than the worst act that he has ever committed.

A Swedish human life group also supported him for much of the time he was on death row. They felt his case was a strong argument for reforming the death penalty. Everyone who knew him, including the warden, and many that didn't know him, supported converting his death sentence to life in prison. After over seventeen years he was a very different man, no longer the young naïve kid who worshipped his mentally ill older brother. I support the death penalty, but this case has given me, and others, second thoughts.

Instead of execution, I recommended the very well-spoken, articulate James to be put in handcuffs and leg chains for show and be allowed to speak in schools to young people as an example about where crime leads. I had no doubt that he would make a lasting impression on many young students as he did with me and many others. Allridge's nearly two decades on death row was sharply beneficial to the many persons he helped. His talk would go something like this:

> I have no excuse for what I have done. I took the life of another human being and deserve to die. I did a horrible thing due to social pressure. All of you will be exposed to temptations at one time in your life as I was. Do not succumb as I did, but flee from any situation that could leave someone killed. Do you know what it is like, every day of your life, facing execution by lethal injection? I have suffered much more that the person I killed. Each day my thought is, "if I only had refused to go with my brother that day….? I had a good home. My father was a career military man. I would have had a good life except for the one mistake that I made."

My professional advice was ignored. He was on death row for almost two decades. Another two decades would allow him to continue doing more good in the world. If his presentations to high school students saved only one life, it would have been an equitable tradeoff.

In his final statement before he was executed, speaking slowly and deliberately, Allridge said, "I'm sorry, I really am. Thank you for forgiving me. I leave you all as I came—in love." Lastly, he asked for forgiveness and expressed his faith and the comfort he was given from his renewed Christian faith during this very difficult time. After knowing him for seventeen years, I have no doubt that he was sincere. On August 26, 2004, at 06:22 p.m., the forty-one-year-old Black man was executed by lethal injection. Several veteran witnesses of past executions remarked that he went to his death with a calmness and peacefulness that they had rarely ever seen before. His fourth court-appointed attorney, on his last call to me, said with some anger, "They fried another one without due process." He never did have a retrial as was his right, and I never testified in his behalf. I know he will be greatly missed.

Piano Wave *by James V. Allridge III*

One of the many pictures he sent me.

February 22, 2023. A Hot Topic: Drinking and Drug Use

My column on drinking touched a nerve in several people who wrote to appreciate my thoughts.

One experience which I feel compelled to relate occurred in a local church. A young very attractive teenager in a wheel chair was lifted up onto the stage at the church by two men. She then, without using notes, told the story of how she became paralyzed from the waist down. She was out drinking on a fun Saturday night with her high school friends. Both she and her boyfriend were stoned. He was driving on a narrow country road when a head-on collision totaled both cars. Taken to the hospital by life-flight in critical condition, she survived but was paralyzed from the waist down. This brief second changed her life forever. Gone was her ability to play sports. Gone was her ability to have children. As an invalid, her chances of a normal marriage were small. Depression set in, as did regret. "If-I-only…" thoughts became her daily companion for months. Her story, more than any other, convinced me of the wisdom of abstinence.

When in college my associates asked if I had ever been drunk. When I answered no, one friend told me, "Don't knock it; you might like it." My response was, "That was what I was afraid of." Knowing my personality, and that of certain family members, I knew I could be led down the road to alcoholism, or at least binge drinking.

When in college, drug use, LSD, *Cannabis* (marijuana/pot/weed), mescaline (peyote), PCP, psilocybin, salvia, and ayahuasca, among others, was a problem. Also in college, when in a sociology class, the issue of drug use came up. I was asked if I have ever been high on drugs. When I answered no, I was told, "Don't condemn drug use if you have never tried it." I explained I get high on music, and drugs was an artificial high. The professor asked if I drove to the college today. I answered yes. He mentioned that driving was also an artificial way of reaching your goal, just as drugs were. Why not walk? It took me an hour to drive, and walking was not possible, I explained. I was not convinced. Later, I worked in a drug treatment house in Detroit and had an opportunity to talk to many users. They were sent there by court order, so the clients were not self-selected. One fact I noticed was the enormously different ways people responded to drugs. One man stated when he smoked marijuana it was like smoking pure air. Nothing. Another man noted that marijuana caused him to go into a paranoia state which, he recognized after the high wore off, caused him to become totally irrational.

Today the problem is a new drug called fentanyl. The fentanyl category of opioids accounted for 53,480 preventable American deaths in the year 2020, representing a 59 percent increase over the 33,725 total the year before. Fentanyl and its salts consist of white granular or crystalline powders. These narcotic analgesics have a potency close to eighty times that of morphine. Fentanyl derivatives include Alfentanil, Remifentanil, Sufentanil, and Carfentanil. They are used in medicine as a safe and effective anesthetic and analgesic. The problem is street drugs are usually not pharmacologically pure. One should never buy a drug from a street vender, even aspirin. These facts must be stressed in our schools and churches to counter the fentanyl craze. The most effective presentation I have ever heard was the young girl's story. We need many more personal testimonies like this in our schools and churches.

March 1, 2023. Toledo Dentist's Crusade Against Aluminum Cookware

I have long been interested in health quacks and cure-alls. Many otherwise intelligent people accept clearly fallacious fads. Part of the reason may be sick people naturally seek a cure, and hope clouds reason. One of the most extreme examples was the almost half-century crusade against the use of aluminum cookware. The movement claimed that aluminum cookware caused serious diseases including cancer.

The primary evidence against aluminum was numerous case histories that claimed those who used aluminum pots and pans soon thereafter developed various maladies. When their cookware was switched to enamel, the victim's health rapidly improved. In a typical case, an article titled "Two More Aluminum Sacrifices" quoted a 1930s Cleveland *Plain Dealer* story about two young children who died from a "mysterious poisoning." The illnesses occurred shortly after they consumed a meal boiled in an aluminum kettle.

The editor concluded that the aluminum cookery caused the poisoning, asking "how many fathers and mothers will be made ill; how many babies slain before the government prevents this unnecessary slaughter by banning all aluminum cooking utensils." No mention was made about an investigation into the deaths. If the parents ate the same food, did they get sick? The actual cause could be due to anything from botulism to rancid food—the family was poor, and possibly the food was contaminated.

Aluminum, although the third most common element in the Earth's crust, was difficult to purify until Oberlin College student Charles M. Hall developed an electrolytic process in 1886 that lowered the cost enormously. The price of aluminum plummeted from ninety dollars per pound to as low as twenty-seven cents per pound in the 1920s. Soon, hundreds of aluminum products became common. Aluminum was an ideal metal for many uses, including cookware, because it is relatively lightweight, able to be shaped easily, and is an excellent heat conductor.

A case Betts used was related by a reader, a Mr. Hanson, who claimed that he used aluminum cookware for years and suffered from "bilious attacks" and would "almost go blind" from an "ice-like film." After he replaced all of his aluminum cooking pots, the blindness disappeared, and he claimed he has felt great ever since.

The writings of Toledo dentist Charles T. Betts (1879–1959) were a primary basis of the over three-decade-long campaign against aluminum. He self-published his many books on the topic, some of which I was able to purchase on the internet. Betts's publications included "Aspirin Poisoning," "Early Grave Via the Modern Kitchen," and "Death in the Pot." He received thousands of letters from all over the world supportive of his work.

Betts also believed that persons under the age of fifteen should not brush their teeth unless they "are ill or in need of medical attention." He argued that, since cats and dogs do not brush after each meal, neither should humans because, he claimed, "brushing causes the diseases of the mouth, now common to our children. After going to a school play we do not wash out our eyes. Thus, after a meal, we do not need to brush our teeth."

Betts, called the North American guru of the anti-aluminum movement, never went to dental school. Instead, he apprenticed with a dentist, as was common then, and was licensed to practice dentistry in Ohio. Dr. Betts's daughter, Bonnie Staffel, mentioned to me that during the Great Depression he provided dental work at no cost or for trade. His daughter stressed her father's ideas must be understood as part of the culture in which he wrote and lived, including, especially, the Depression (1929–1939). The anti-aluminum movement was part of the wider popular culture trend against orthodox medicine that stressed using "natural foods" to treat illness and eschewed what they regarded as "unnatural remedies" such as pharmaceutical drugs. In the early 1920s, allopathic medicine was widely regarded as a lowly trade in which cures were rare and scientific understanding of disease was even rarer.

Dr. Morris Fishbein, a popular author and a former head of the American Medical Association, evaluated Dr. Betts's claims. His assessment is as accurate today as it was in 1927. In his words, research has shown "the cooking even of acid fruits and vegetables for long periods of time resulted only in the slightest traces of aluminum in the juice. The theory of the Toledo dentist is pernicious in that it is used to disseminate false advice concerning cancer." All of us have opinions that lie outside of our area of expertise. Even informed intelligent people sometimes pontificate on areas they know very little about. The history of the opposition to aluminum cookware eloquently demonstrates much about the need to be constrained by the limits of one's knowledge. It also helps to listen to others' opinions and read both sides.

March 8, 2023. The Importance of Apologetics

The feedback from my previous columns includes, "I would hope that every church teaches morals." True, but this is not the only important ingredient required for church survival: Another critical factor is apologetics. Apologetics is literally a study of the defense of the Christian faith. The Greek word *apologia* means "defense." In every generation, people face the challenges, questions, and concerns about the gospel message of the Christian faith.

This challenge must be met if the church is to survive. Numerous surveys by both secular and Christian research organizations find the major reason young person's abandon Christianity is that they do not believe, or that they have major doubts, about the truth of the Bible, thus Christianity. My upbringing effectively dealt with this by including apologetics as a major part of our Bible study. One important fact to keep in mind is that the Bible is history, and much of it can be corroborated by secular history books. Most of these are not used as studies in place of the Bible but as references to give historical background and support to Scripture.

Critical sources include Flavius Josephus, a first-century Romano-Jewish historian who defected to the Romans' side and was granted Roman citizenship. He became an advisor and friend of Vespasian's son, Titus, and a professional Roman historian. His writings are the chief source, next to the Bible, for the details of the history of ancient Israel. They provide a significant independent, extra-biblical account of Pontius Pilate, Herod the Great, John the Baptist, and the world of Jesus of Nazareth.

Another important source is Archbishop James Ussher's 1,300 page *The Annals of the World*. Ussher (1581–1656), a meticulous researcher and compiler, correlated the events in Genesis with secular human history. He supported his work with over twelve thousand footnotes from secular sources. Many of the references available when Ussher was working on his book in the 1600s are now lost to history. He began writing *The Annals* when he was thirteen and spent the rest of his life researching for his *tour de force*.

Another important book is *The Book of Jubilees* written in Hebrew in the middle of the second century BC, first translated into Greek, then into Latin. It addresses the history of the Creation and of Israel up to Exodus 12:50. The goal of the book was to answer, and also to explain, questions left unanswered in Genesis. It also was written to respond to attacks on the veracity of the Bible by both pagan Greeks and skeptical Jews. At the time *The Book of Jubilees* was written, Greek philosophy was thriving and challenged Jewish beliefs, especially the book of Genesis.

The Book of Jubilees also covers salient details about the beginning of the human race, the source of Jewish laws going back to the ancient beginning, and how demons, Satan, and angels fit into creation. It is considered canonical by the

Ethiopian Orthodox Church and Ethiopian Jews. Although not considered part of the canon by most Christian churches, it strongly supports the Bible and adds useful background information to the biblical narrative.

Also very important are 1 and 2 Maccabees, which are early Jewish writings detailing the history of the Jews in the first century BC. These books are part of the canon of the Greek Orthodox, Roman Catholic, Coptic, and Russian Orthodox churches but are not recognized as canonical by Protestants and Jews. Nonetheless, they are found in many Protestant Bibles and are an important source of the background of Bible events. The books outline the history of the Jewish leaders called the Maccabees. The first book portrays the effort by the Jews to regain their cultural and religious independence from the Roman emperor Antiochus IV Epiphanes after his desecration of the Jewish temple.

Highly recommended for study are books including *The Case for Christ*, *The Case for Faith*, and others by Lee Strobel. The classics, *Evidence that Demands a Verdict* by Josh McDowell and *The Bible as History* by Werner Keller and Joachim Rohork, are also very important.

For more in-depth study, critical are the *Ante-Nicene Fathers*. This set of ten volumes consists of the writings of the early church fathers until AD 325. Lastly, at least for reference, are the writings of many early historians who wrote at the time of Christ. The most respected include Herodotus, who is called "The Father of History," and also Thucydides, Xenophon, Polybius, and most importantly, Tacitus. As 1 Peter 3:15 admonishes, "Always be prepared to give an answer to everyone who asks you to give the reason for the hope that you have."

March 15, 2023. Some Pioneers Make Foolish Mistakes

I always welcome feedback from readers, which often can be very helpful. I recently received a letter from Dr. Betts's grandson, Ben Locke. He correctly noted that I need to provide greater context to my article on Betts to better understand the first half of the twentieth century when Dr. Betts lived. The scientific community's involvement in public health and the technology used to protect public health were, compared to today, grossly lacking. Mr. Locke gave as an example the scandals of the meat-packing industries, which were exposed by Upton Sinclair in his book *The Jungle*, a mere five years after Dr. Betts published his book *Aluminum Poisoning*. Sinclair's vivid description of diseased, rotten, and contaminated meat shocked the public and led to the modern federal food safety laws.

Another example is the American government undertaking a project involving syphilitic Black males at Tuskegee, Alabama that lasted for forty years. Treatment was available but not administered because the researchers wanted to determine if the progression of syphilis was different in Black males as compared to White males. They found the obvious, namely that there was no difference in the way the disease progressed based on one's skin melanin content.

Ben Locke also noted that, to determine shoe fit, the unregulated use of X-ray fluoroscopes by shoe stores was common. Physicians also used X-rays to shrink enlarged thyroid glands in babies. Now we know that radiation exposure to the thyroid at a young age is a long-term risk factor for the development of differentiated thyroid cancer. In some respects, Dr. Betts was a pioneer, one of the first medical practitioners asking serious questions about toxicity.

My favorite example is the discovery that X-rays produce mutations which then, and now, are the major means evolution relies on to produce genetic variety. For evolution to work, genetic variety is critical. No genetic variety, no evolution. Darwin correctly recognized that natural selection was valid (due to its being a tautology, a self-evident truth): the more fit are more likely to survive and have offspring. However, he never could come up with a theory explaining the *origin* of new genetic variations.

In 1903, Dutch geneticist Hugo de Vries discovered mutations that caused sporadic, sudden changes in living organisms. Then, in the 1920's, Dr. Hermann J. Muller discovered that X-rays could increase the mutation rate by as much as one hundred times. Muller reasoned that by creating mutations using X-rays, he could drastically speed up evolution. A March 1928 *Scientific American* article announced his discovery to the world: "New Discovery Speeds Up Evolution." For his discovery, Muller was awarded the most prestigious award in science, the Nobel Prize. In his 1946 Nobel lecture, Muller wrote that "this accumulation of many rare, mainly tiny changes is the chief means of artificial animal and plant improvement, and is …[how] natural evolution has occurred guided by natural selection. Thus the Darwinian theory becomes implemented."

Now we know that the vast majority of mutations are harmful. My cancer research experience taught me how and why mutations are a major cause of disease, including cancer, cystic fibrosis, Huntington's disease, sickle-cell disease, Down syndrome, and over seven thousand other diseases. In short, we need to have more respect for the early pioneers of our society in spite of some of what we now recognize as foolish mistakes.

March 29, 2023. The Scopes Monkey Trial Myth

One of the most distorted historical events in American history was the Scopes "Monkey" Trial. Professor Giberson claims the Scopes trial is "probably the best-known legal confrontation in history." The common conclusion goes something like the following *History Channel* claim: "The Scopes Trial, also known as the Scopes Monkey Trial, was the 1925 prosecution of science teacher John Scopes for teaching evolution in a Tennessee public school, which a recent bill had made illegal." In fact, the bill only prohibited teaching *human* evolution, not evolution.

One reason many Christians believed that teaching human evolution was a problem because, in the 1920s, one of the major proofs of human evolution was the existence of what was then widely believed to be inferior human races, specifically Blacks. The Bible is clear. There is only one race, the human race.

John Scope used a biology textbook titled *Hunter's Civic Biology* which openly taught racism. Examples include the following statement: "there exist upon the Earth five races or varieties of man, each very different from the other … the highest type of all, the Caucasians, represented by the civilized white inhabitants of Europe and America." Hunter then added that we can improve the human race by: "The science of being well-born called *eugenics*."

Harvard law professor Alan Dershowitz noted that the eugenics movement "took its impetus from Darwin's theory of natural selection." Dershowitz correctly noted persons actively advocating evolution in 1925, when the Scopes trial occurred, included "racists, militarists, and nationalists" who used evolution "to push some pretty horrible programs," including forced sterilizations of putative "inferior people." Darwin explained in detail how a race with superior qualities, those selected by natural selection, would normally destroy the weaker, less-evolved, races. When natural selection ceases, evolution also ceases. Hitler stressed this point repeatedly in his book titled *Mein Kampf* (meaning "*My Struggle*" or "*My Battle*").

William Jennings Bryan volunteered to argue in court for the prosecution in the Scopes trial. A major concern of Bryan was the degradation of humans by the racism motivated by evolution. Bryan's belief was that all humans are the offspring of the first human couple, Adam and Eve. Thus, all humans are of the same race, the human race. Evolution, on the other hand, as the Hunter text illustrated, requires racial differences for survival of the fittest to function. If all humans are equal, evolution cannot work. The Hunter text illustrated Bryan's concern for the reason that it was "laced with the racism of the day." For this correct observation, Bryan has been maligned ever since. Derided as a "fundamentalist," he was actually a liberal Democrat. He ran three times for President as a Democrat and was defeated each time by Republicans.

Professor Marvin Olasky observed that "Hunter's view of eugenics, widely accepted early in the twentieth century, was a common deduction drawn from and associated with Darwinian theory." Hunter openly advocated the solution to what he saw as the main social problem in society, namely genetically inferior persons. Many Tennesseans, especially African Americans, also objected to the *implications* of the entire evolutionary doctrine that were made explicit in the Hunter science textbook that was required by their state. The Hunter text actually taught that it was our civic duty to apply eugenics to achieve racial improvement.

As Scopes trial historian Tontonoz concluded, "Eugenics was quickly becoming a scientific religion in America: this was the context in which Bryan opposed the teaching of evolution in public schools." It is clear from his writings that Bryan was very concerned about racism and eugenics, and this concern was a major reason why he opposed teaching human evolution. Thus, in the 1920s, Bryan's opposers were fighting to maintain, not only the teaching of racism in the public schools, but also the preservation of racism and eugenics in American society. In fact, in his study of the trial, author Dennis Sewell wrote: "The Scopes Monkey Trial was more about racism, not God. Almost everything we think we know about the Dayton spectacle is wrong."

April 5, 2023. A Murderer Freed

One of the most interesting cases I have ever worked on when employed at the Oakland County court was about a man in his late seventies that I will call William. He owned a company that designed and manufactured scientific instruments for his clients in the Detroit area. When he retired, he set up a large man-cave with his precision tools and equipment, such as his drill press and lathe, in the basement of his Bloomfield Hills, Michigan, home. After he lost his wife of almost a half century, he married Martha.

Although a well-to-do gentleman, he was wise about spending money and had no need to be frugal. His new wife experienced the opposite upbringing and life. She was from a poor family and had to be frugal to a fault. When his son from his first marriage was appointed dean at the college where he was a professor, Martha adamantly refused to allow her husband to spend money at a nice restaurant when his son and his son's wife visited them in Bloomfield Hills to celebrate. They ended up having carryout from the local McDonalds.

Martha's obsession with money got worse each year of their marriage. William enjoyed a homemade milkshake several times a week, and Martha insisted he use a plastic straw which could be washed and reused. Eventually, Martha insisted he sell all of his precision tools and invest the money. Making things with his tools was his life. As he was placing his workshop equipment in their three-car garage to sell, he totally lost control, probably for the first time in his life. His pent-up rage let loose, resulting in striking his wife several times on the head, killing her.

He then called the police using the phone in the garage and sat on a lawn chair in the large yard of their five-bedroom home. While sitting on the lawn chair in the sun, when the police arrived, they thought he was an old senile man making up a story about what happened. When they saw her lifeless body on the garage floor, they changed their mind about the old man's story. He was arrested and charged with murder. Soon friends and neighbors came out in the defense of the quiet, self-spoken man who was about five feet six inches tall and weighed less than 150 pounds. His supporters, many who worked for him for decades, claimed they never saw this devoted life-long Christian Scientist church member angry. His pre-sentence investigation concluded that, although he faced a very difficult life with his second wife, he successfully kept in his anger during his entire five-year marriage until the loss of his basement workshop caused the fit of rage within him to momentarily explode.

His faith prevented William from divorcing Martha and forced him to adjust the best he could in an intolerable situation that he endured for over five years. When he came to the probation office on 1200 North Telegraph Road in Pontiac, Michigan, he wore a conservative suit and carried a brief case. Several clerks at first thought he was an attorney, not an accused murderer. At the trial, before the judge sat a man close to eighty years old with not so much as a parking ticket. His sentence was, said the judge, "life with his conscience." He responded that that was the worst sentence possible he could have. The judge reasoned that sentencing an eighty-year-old man that posed no threat to the community to prison served no purpose. Some felt that William went through a lot the last few years and would not likely survive a long sentence given for those who murder. He died a few years later.

April 12, 2023. Why Eisenhower Hated War but Fought the Nazis

The theme of my new book on Dwight David "Ike" Eisenhower was that World War II was essentially a war between creation and evolution, and the creation side won. If the evolution side had prevailed, a large swath of the population would not be here, and those who remained would all be speaking German: "kannst du Deutsch sprechen?"

From his youth, the Eisenhower family read and reread the Bible from cover to cover. Much of the Bible, Ike realized, is history. In the Bible, Ike read about the second king of the Babylonian Empire, King Nebuchadnezzar II, plus Julius Caesar, Pontius Pilate, and many other historical figures. The family owned several college books on history which Ike read to learn more about the Bible events. In short, Ike got hooked on history. His Abilene High School (Abilene, Kansas 1906–1909) 1909 yearbook predicted he would become a history professor at Yale. Instead of teaching history, he made history.

A focus of the Bible student group he was part of was apologetics, emphasizing why human evolution was false because God created the first man and women. This topic greatly impressed the young Ike. When serving as the Supreme Allied Commander of the Allied Expeditionary Force in Europe, he achieved the five-star rank as a General. Ike's large, well-trained intelligence gathering team helped him to understand that the ultimate Nazi war goals were rooted in social Darwinian doctrine. He learned that the genocide of the Jews, Slavs, and other persons that the Nazi's deemed were members of inferior races was the culmination of a decade of German policy under Nazi rule. Extermination of all inferior races was the ultimate goal of the Nazi dictator, Adolf Hitler, and the Nazi Party. In short, their priority was genocide based on race, not conquest. The Nazi goal was for those they considered the superior race, the Aryan race, to dominate the world. Eventually, the inferior races, all non-Aryans, would be annihilated, creating a better world for all mankind, or so they taught.

As a creationist, Eisenhower believed all men were descended from Adam, thus all humans were related by blood. There was only one race, the human race. This realization drove Ike to defeat the Nazis no matter what the cost. He once said he hated war, but he hated the Nazi evolutionary/racist belief even more. When Germany was finally defeated, Ike, with good reason, feared that the fact of the Holocaust would be denied by many, so he launched the most extensive documentation program in history to document what happened in Nazi Germany and why. Thousands of interviews were completed, and several large film crews labored to carefully document the Holocaust travesties. Lastly, a mammoth depository to store the documentation was established. The anti-God fruit of social Darwinism was documented so that all men could proclaim "never again" to the Holocaust.

April 19, 2023. Anatomically Correct Dolls

One of my most beneficial experiences testifying in court involved a child molestation case. I was flown to Tennessee and met with the accused molester, whom I will call Timothy, who was then living with his mother. He was then going through a divorce, and his soon to be ex-wife was living in the family home with their two children, both then under three. Timothy's mother was a widow who lived in the family home, a large, older, stately home. Timothy was forced to live with his mother because of the heavy financial costs he had to pay in order to legally defend himself from the molestation charges. The state was paying all of his wife's expenses.

I previously had had long phone conversations with him, and he sent me copies of the extensive court and family services reports that provided a good background of his case. His now deceased father was a prominent doctor, and none of his siblings had a police record. Timothy and his mother were dumbfounded over the claim made by his ex-wife that he had been sexually molesting his two children for many months. I have to admit, although I had worked with a variety of persons who were involved in what were then regarded as sexual perversions, I could not comprehend how a father could sexually molest his own young children. I never saw the children. They were with his ex-wife's mother during all of the court proceedings.

The main evidence of the molestation was the anatomically correct dolls which were used to reach an admission of molestation that was repeated by the children to the judge in his chambers. Anatomically detailed dolls are made of plastic or cotton and come dressed with easily removable clothing. Both male and female gonads, as well as their apertures, are present on the dolls.

In court, when waiting for our case to be heard by the judge, the social workers became aware of who I was and why I was there. They spared no words of contempt for me, wondering how I could defend what they described as a sick child molester. I said nothing but was, at this point, very apprehensive about this case. When our case was called into court, I was the first person to be put on the witness stand for the defense. My testimony was critical. After reviewing my qualifications, I was sworn in as an expert witness. As this case was many years ago, I remember few details about my testimony but do vividly remember spending twenty or thirty minutes on the stand, most of this time involved in a dialogue with the judge.

I had never had this experience before. All other times the dialogue was between me and the client's and prosecutor's lawyers. I was very impressed by this judge. He was openly very concerned about why these small children would admit being molested when, as we alleged, it never happened. I suggested letting the father visit with his children under the close supervision of someone the judge could trust and then interview the children again in the judge's chambers. A few weeks later, after several supervised visits with the father, the children were again interviewed. They again indicated they were molested, confirming my belief that the use of anatomically correct dolls to obtain evidence of molestation were unreliable. The judge then allowed the father to play a role in the lives of his children.

Several similar court cases later came to the same conclusion. When this trial was held, the use of anatomically correct dolls to convict men of sexual molestation was a new trend. Professionals often assumed that children did not lie about sexual abuse and could not be "coached" to make false statements about important events such as sexual abuse. It was soon determined that coercive questioning and suggestive interview techniques could produce serious errors in a child's statements. Too often using these props to interview young children provide more *inaccurate* details than children not given the dolls.

The controversy over the dolls led to some courts banning use of information in court obtained in interviews when the dolls were used. Even before this, it was recognized that young children were suggestible and vulnerable to making serious errors in their testimony. If the child is instructed to "pretend" when using the dolls, this instruction may trigger the child to moving into a fantasy world. Although adults attempt to use the dolls to overcome a young child's verbal limitations, they may instead increase the likelihood of leading the children to make misleading statements. I was proud to have played a small role in the reevaluation of certain tactics that caused convictions of persons unjustly accused of child molestation.

April 26, 2023. The IRS Plan to Spend Your Money

The IRS operating plan proposed spending tens of billions of dollars to audit wealthy taxpayers and corporations. The $80 billion in new funding the Biden administration procured will also be used to increase enforcement efforts. I have to wonder if they can collect enough new taxes to offset the $80 billion-costs. Most wealthy taxpayers and large corporations hire lawyers and tax professionals, often ex-IRS agents, to do their taxes. Each side will likely spend a lot of time and money in court.

If the IRS prevails, businesses will be forced to lower operating costs to pay for the higher tax by raising the price of their products and services. Or they will lay off workers, and/or ship even more jobs to China, and/or shut down the less profitable parts of their business. Another option is closing some under-producing stores, often those in poor neighborhoods or those in "the hood." Likely some combination of these options will be employed. Some businesses will go out of business, causing many thousands of workers to lose their jobs. If forced to file bankruptcy, workers may also lose their retirement and health insurance. Bankruptcy cases now average thirteen thousand annually.

All businesses must turn a profit to stay in business. And the first obligation of all businesses is *to stay in business*. The enormous profits that make the news are required to offset the previous year's losses that are part of doing business. Lawsuits are a major expense, now costing corporations billions. Note the advertisements recruiting persons to file claims who have used some product and suffered from cancer or Alzheimer's. They only state that their product is *linked* to cancer or *may cause* cancer. They rarely say their product *directly causes* cancer. One of the many companies forced to pay out billions from lawsuits includes the German company Bayer AG, producer of the glyphosate-based pesticide *Roundup* that has so far paid out $11 billion. Glyphosate, which has a lower acute toxicity rate to humans than 94% of all herbicides, is the number one weed killer used throughout the world. Thus, some users will, in terms of probability, due to a myriad of causes, develop cancer or Alzheimer's. In court, widows of lung-cancer husbands can easily get a sympathetic jury to award them a large amount of money. Juries reason this is small change for a billion-dollar corporation. Bayer has now won five court cases based on four decades of scientific studies concluding that Roundup can be used safely and is noncarcinogenic. Nonetheless, Bayer will stop selling glyphosate-based weed killers in the US residential market, which accounts for the "vast majority" of lawsuits, but will continue to sell it to farmers, who use enormous amounts of it. The company also reached a deal to settle most of the roughly one hundred thousand then-pending Roundup lawsuits for nearly $10 billion. A corporation can be innocent and still have to pay out multibillions.

In 2021, Johnson & Johnson paid out $2 billion due to a verdict in favor of women who claimed they developed ovarian cancer from their talc products. They set aside nearly $9 billion to settle talc powder lawsuits. Yet, talc is accepted as safe for use in personal-care products throughout the world, and Roundup is still widely considered the safest herbicide in the world.

On the average, half of all hospitals are facing one or more lawsuits each year. Over half of licensed US physicians have been sued. The result is medical malpractice insurance costs hospitals between $4,000 and $12,000 per year for each general practice physician. For surgeons, the yearly cost is from $30,000 to $50,000. Obstetricians pay very high malpractice insurance premiums due to the risk inherent in birth and delivery. About 1 percent of all children have birth defects, many wrongly blamed on the doctor. The lawsuit award can total up to $120,000 because the two-year statute of limitations in many states doesn't end until the baby turns eighteen. Thus, care must be paid for by the doctor's insurance for eighteen years. This is all the cost of doing business.

Much of the money to run most businesses comes from stockholders. Retirement systems income often comes from investing money in company stocks; thus, most of us have a stake in the success of corporations. And if they do not perform well, investments flow to those that do. In short, if the IRS gets more billions from corporations, it may cause much more harm to society as a whole than if it did not get the money.

May 3, 2023. Galileo's Persecution Myth

Myths, once they get started, have a life of their own that can last for generations. One of these myths is that the church persecuted Galileo because he rejected geocentricism, the idea that the sun goes around the Earth, and accepted heliocentrism, the belief that the Earth goes around the sun. It is more accurate to conclude that, although many Jesuits and other clerics opposed Galileo, the main opponents of the idea that the Earth circles the sun were academicians teaching science in the universities. Conversely, much, if not most, of Galileo's support came from church officials. Official Catholic doctrine established by the Council of Trent concluded that the Bible was only without error in matters of faith or morals, not statements that may be used to defend some astronomy idea.

"So, why did so many scientists oppose Galileo?"

The real threat Galileo posed to the contemporary scientists were not his heliocentric views, but his insistence that, to understand reality, science should not rely on popular authority, but rather on analytic inductive observation, research, and experimentation. A major reason for the academic opposition to Galileo was from the various "natural" philosophers. The reason was because these philosophies were firmly based on Aristotelian doctrine derived from the works of the Greek philosopher Aristotle (384–322 BC) who taught Ptolemaic geocentrism.

"But didn't Galileo have the scientific evidence on his side?"

No. He didn't have solid scientific support. Galileo's favorite proof was his conclusion that the Earth's rotational motion alone caused the high- and low-tide movement like the sloshing of water in a moving bathtub. Thus, the Earth must be moving and is not stationary as geocentricism taught. This argument was completely wrong because Galileo's theory would produce only a single tide each day. As any of his Venetian friends could have told him, two tides occur for each twenty-four-hour day. So, while Galileo was ultimately correct about heliocentrism, he was wrong to believe that he had scientific proof.

"Why, then, would the church officials oppose Galileo?"

The academics were furious at Galileo for opposing the most eminent scientist of his day, Ptolemy. They called Galileo names such as a "braggart of an anti-Aristotelianism" and were angry that he was allowed to openly promote his iconoclastic views. Many were jealous of the royal treatment that Galileo was given by the church. They also resented his large salary and the continual special favors bestowed on him by the Grand Duke.

Galileo's main problem was his rash indiscretion, his overbearing personality, and his insistence on presenting his ideas to the common people by writing in the common tongue about ideas that were far from being settled, much as evolutionists do today. The proper approach would have been to write well-documented scholarly papers in Latin and then wait patiently for the scholarly appraisal.

"Don't scientists need to first confirm their ideas by good and careful research and only then present them to the public?"

Very true. Frustrated by trying to disprove Galileo with scientific arguments, his detractors decided that it was easier to silence him on the grounds of heresy. In the end, the church was used by the academic community to squelch what some academicians felt was the threat Galileo posed to both their method of obtaining knowledge and to their authority.

"What was the other side's view?"

Some Jesuit astronomers, in contrast, were willing to look through his telescope and saw the evidence for themselves. This evidence included the revolution of Jupiter's four largest moons, today called the Galilean moons, around the giant planet. As a result, they became convinced that what Galileo claimed about some of his astronomical observations was true. So, they honored Galileo. After all, he was a Jesuit-trained scientist whose fame brought honor and prestige to the Jesuit order.

"Wasn't Galileo tried by the church and found guilty of heresy?"

In fact, Galileo was never charged with, nor tried for, heresy, as commonly believed. Heresy was a far more serious offense that carried a much stiffer penalty. Galileo was tried, and found guilty, only of not keeping the agreement he made in 1616 with Cardinal Bellarmine to present heliocentrism as a hypothetical idea until definitive scientific proof was found. Many historians believe that the document supporting their 1616 claim was a forgery or a draft. It was not signed by Galileo or Bellarmine, the latter of whom was no longer alive when Galileo's trial commenced in 1633.

"So, his enemies used the church to silence him?"

The Catholic Church's major sin was capitulating to the pressure from the scientific community and the enemies of Galileo. Only as a result of pressure from both the secular establishment, plus the support of the Aristotelian philosophers, did the church side against Galileo. They knew they could not get a heresy charge to stick, so they got the seventy-year-old on failing to keep his word to treat heliocentrism as theory as he promised, until scientific proof was established.

Another mistake Galileo made was to write a book that pictured his good friend, Cardinal Barberini, as a dim-witted defender of Ptolemy called Simplicio. Barberini was a mathematician by training and a university professor by profession. When he became Pope, he took the name Urban VIII. Any scholarly book on Galileo provides the documentation for this sketch of the Galileo affair. I have forty-seven in my library. Yet the myth of Galileo persecuted by the Catholic Church still thrives to this day, almost four hundred years after the event. It survives only because many secularists find it useful to support the false narrative that Christianity has for centuries opposed science.

May 10, 2023. Blessed Are the Peacemakers

On a plaque in a German Lutheran church I visited was a long list of men who were members of that church that died in World War II. The oak plaque imprinted with gold letters said, "zu Ehren der tapferen Männer, die bei der Verteidigung des Vaterlandes starben," which translated in English is "in honor of the brave men who died defending the Fatherland." I was later told about one brave German Nazi soldier who died while frantically firing when he ran into a group of Americans, knowing he would be killed. He killed fifteen American soldiers and badly wounded several more. He was later lauded as a hero by the German government. Some American soldiers did the same thing, only killing German soldiers.

This behavior does not support our Creator's goal, as stated in Isaiah 2:4 which says, "And he shall judge among the nations, and shall rebuke many people: and they shall beat their swords into plowshares, and their spears into pruninghooks: nation shall not lift up sword against nation, neither shall they learn war anymore." In the New Testament, war is universally seen as evil, and Jesus over and over emphasized peace. He advised us to avoid retaliation and revenge and to extend our love even to our enemies:

> You have heard that it was said, "Eye for eye, and tooth for tooth." But I tell you…if someone strikes you on the right cheek, turn to him the other also. And if someone wants to sue you and take your tunic, let him have your cloak as well. If someone forces you to go one mile, go with him two miles. …You have heard that it was said, "Love your neighbor and hate your enemy." But I tell you: Love your enemies and pray for those who persecute you, that you may be sons of your Father in heaven. (Matt. 5:38−45).

The apostle Paul and other New Testament writers expanded on Jesus' sentiment, writing:

> Never pay back evil for evil to anyone. Respect what is right in the sight of all men. If possible, so far as it depends on you, be at peace with all men. Never take your own revenge, beloved, but leave room for the wrath of God, for it is written, "Vengeance is Mine, I will repay," says the Lord. "But if your enemy is hungry, feed him, and if he is thirsty, give him a drink; for in so doing you will heap burning coals upon his head." Do not be overcome by evil, but overcome evil with good. (Rom. 12:17−21)

When the mob came to arrest Jesus, one of His followers tried to defend Him with a sword. But Jesus rebuked him: "Put your sword back into its place; for all those who take up the sword shall perish by the sword" (Matt. 26:52–53). Surveys have shown, which I agree with, that the war against Nazi Germany was more justified than almost every war fought by Americans during the last century. Jesus said that war is inevitable and will continue until He returns (Mark 13:7–8). Nonetheless, the scriptural teaching is clear: "Blessed are the peacemakers, for it is they that will be children of God" (Matt. 5:9).

Almost all nations on both sides in the European theater of World War I and World War II were nominal Christian nations. The only war that is sanctioned by the scriptures is defensive, not offensive. The leading Russian Orthodox bishop supports the Russian invasion of Ukraine as do most of the Russian people. For support, the Russian government attempts to make it sound like the war was defensive. This is what Hitler did with Czechoslovakia to enable his country to support the war. Many people go to war because they are drafted, not because they believe in the cause. Nonetheless, the Amish, Mennonites, Quakers, Seventh-day Adventists, Jehovah's Witnesses, Christadelphians, Doukhobors, Moravians, and many other Christian sects have taken a firm stand against war based on Christian principles. They will often even go to prison rather than to war. Fortunately, America and other enlightened nations allow alternative service for conscientious objectors, such as hospital work or as a medic in the army.

May 17, 2023. The Mother I Knew

My mother, Irene Buck Bergman, was born November 27, 1920, in Meade, Kansas, and died on September 12, 1996, at age 75. The last decade of her life she suffered from both Parkinson's and Alzheimer's diseases. I now regret that I did not spend more time with her when she was with us. Consequently, I know very little about her early life.

The few details about my mother come from published family histories. Her mother, Mamie, died in childbirth at age twenty-nine, forcing the family of three girls and two boys to rear themselves. The girls did all of the housework, including cleaning and cooking, and helped raise their two brothers. My maternal grandfather, Benjamín Buck, a blacksmith, came to the United States from Hamburg, Germany, in the early 1900s.

Mother was baptized and confirmed in St. John Lutheran Church. As an active and adventuresome young lady of fifteen, she learned to drive her bother Norman's car. While in school, in addition to the academic curriculum, she learned to sew and type. After school she worked at the Lakeway Hotel to help support the struggling family.

After graduating from Meade High School, because not many employment opportunities existed in the small town of Meade, all three sisters ended up in Detroit. Detroit was then a booming city due to its vibrant war industry, supporting World War II building tanks, guns, and planes. Soon after arriving in Detroit, my mother met my father when she worked in a dental office where he was a patient. They married in 1943 and divorced sixteen years later when I was in junior high school.

Mother then had to struggle to support us. Her first step was to get a full-time job. She was hired by Consumers Power Company at the starting wage of fifty-four dollars a week. She worked her way up to the special ledger department handling multimillion-dollar accounts until she elected to retire a year early due to the onset of Alzheimer's in her early sixties. Mom never remarried, although dated several men; most were divorced and had their own problems, especially alcoholism. It was not easy for a divorced woman in her forties with three boys to find a good man and remarry then.

One memory I have of my mother, although confirmed as a Lutheran, sent my older brother and me to the nearest church. It was a conservative Bible church only a block away from us, on the corner of Greenfield Avenue and 13 Mile Road in Royal Oak, Michigan. We attended only once, but this one visit had a profound effect on me. When my father, a nonbeliever, learned about our church visit, an aggressive argument resulted. That was the last time we attended a church until my parents divorced in 1959.

My mother's whole life was her three boys; my older brother, Ron, me, and my younger brother, Mike. Every Saturday she did the washing with an old Maytag ringer washer and hung the clothes up to dry outside. When it was too cold outside, she hung them in the basement to dry. It took most of the day to wash the clothes for the four of us. To get everything done her day began at 5:30 am and ended at 10:00 pm. She served home cooked meals for us during most of our childhood and adolescence; no fast food or TV dinners. We went out to eat, at most, three times a year. We assumed mothers were supposed to cook, clean, wash our clothes, pay the bills, make sure we got to school on time, and take us to the doctor. The house was always spotless. It is now, as an adult, that I fully realize how much she sacrificed for us.

Those of you who have a mother still living should learn some of the details of her life, her hopes and dreams, her best and worst days, her childhood highlights and memories, pets, boyfriends, marriage milestones, and life in general growing up and growing old. It is too late for me to really know about my mother's past. Ideally, I should have done a memory book, as my wife did with her family, the Haldimans, where each member wrote a few pages about their life. The life sketches in the book were assembled with many pictures. We made copies of it and gave them to our children.

In short, my mother had a profound influence on me, which I am today very grateful for. Most importantly, she taught me the need to work hard, to get a good education, to do the best I could with the life God gave me, to be kind to everyone and think evil of no one. She also helped us understand the harm done by drinking and smoking, habits none of us ever took up, largely due to her example. Learn as much as possible about your mother if you still can. The time you have with her on Earth is all too short.

May 24, 2023. Why Some Churches Grow and Others Die

Since I have been involved in the apologetics ministry I have spoken at over six hundred churches, ranging from thirty to three thousand members. I have consistently noted numerous practices in common in growing churches. Their main emphasis is the firm acceptance of the Word and works of God. Another common factor is that they have scrapped most of the ritual liturgy common in the mainline Protestant churches. One important trend is to make the service less formal and involve the congregation more in the service, a trait close to universal in Black churches. The name of the church is also very important. Terms like Bryan Bible Church, Bryan Community Church, or Bryan Christian Fellowship are recommended. Avoid mainline domination names including Episcopalian, Lutheran, Methodist, or Presbyterian.

Music is critical, and the key is variety, not loudness or repetition. Often used for special music are congregation members, local talent, and occasionally students learning to play an instrument. Other critical components, besides apologetics, are sermons on the principles of biblical interpretation (hermeneutics), the study of future things and end times (eschatology), the study of Christ and salvation (soteriology), the study of purpose and the design intent of the Creator (teleology), and the history of the Bible and reasons to explain and support the Christian faith. A sermon on the Bible and health has been one of the most well-received sermons in my repertoire. Both the Hebrew and Greek scriptures provide excellent guidance for not only spiritual health but also mental and physical health.

Most also stress confronting the anti-Christian culture, as was the norm in the early first-century church. This means delivering biblically based sermons on current social problems to help church members in their Christian walk. Contemporary issues the church is forced to confront today, include drugs, immorality, materialism, adultery, fornication, homosexuality, divorce, cults, marriage, war, and appropriate Christian behavior supporting the song "They Will Know We Are Christians By Our Love." Community involvement is also important, not only helping feed the poor and other Christian works but involvement in the community supporting the schools and the proper education of students. Some churches even invite persons running for the school board and/or other public positions, such as judges or the Senate/House representatives, to address the congregation.

One method critical in our visual age is to augment sermons with PowerPoint. Sleeping in church is rarely an issue when we use audio-visual enhancements. PowerPoint is universally used in schools, business presentations, and, likewise, increasingly in churches. All of my over fifty apologetic sermons are in PowerPoint, and it is a rare church that does not have a PowerPoint projector system. Some churches even act out sketches to teach biblical events. One of the best examples I have witnessed is the woman caught in adultery, recorded in John 8:3–11, acted out by several talented church members. The youth especially mentioned afterwards how they have now, for the first time, fully understood the impact and meaning behind this parable.

Lastly, some churches interview each family attending the church, either recorded (which is best because it can be edited) or in person in front of the church to help the congregation get to better know their fellow parishioners. This works well even for small congregations. Typical questions asked inquired about their faith, their Christian walk, their background, likes, dislikes, hobbies, where and when they met their spouse, their children, and key events in their life, including losses due to death and illnesses. As one pastor mentioned to me, many churches now dying deserve to die. The church must, besides leading persons to salvation, help the believers live a Christian life.

May 31, 2023. A Visit from a *New York Times* Reporter

One afternoon when I was living in Bowling Green I heard the doorbell ring. As I looked outside, I noticed a woman in her mid-forties. Thinking it was someone collecting money for some cause, I asked if I could help her. She said she was a reporter for *The New York Times* and wondered if she could talk to me. I said yes and invited her in. Talking to reporters was not unusual for me, but they rarely came to my home.

She explained she was the wife of an inmate I knew when I worked in the prison. A number of the inmates told her, "You must meet Dr. Bergman before you go home to New York." They gave her my address and, after she left the prison in Jackson, Michigan, she stopped by to meet me. One of the first questions I asked her was why her husband was in prison. She mentioned she interviewed him for a story several years ago and a long correspondence ensued. After several visits she married him. It was a hard decision and, she explained, one she has never regretted.

I did not remember talking to him, but then I had come to know several dozen inmates whose stories were in many ways similar. Over 70 percent of the inmates were black, and it never occurred to me to ask her if her husband was black to help me identify him in my mind. I did ask her why she married an inmate. She exclaimed she loved her job, which involved traveling all over the world. Her lifestyle ended her first marriage. I mentioned that many inmates exploited women who live on the outside because women friends were a significant source of money for them. She recognized that fact but countered that she was very successful at her work partly because she had learned to read people in spite of their words.

I learned later, after reading a few of her articles, that she was an unusually talented writer. She told me, "I value being married to someone who truly loves me and is not going to be unfaithful as my first husband was," adding,

> He is safe in prison and is not going to be untrue to me, a value that is very important to me. As I travel the world, I know my husband is with me in spirit. I have very good feelings about him and our marriage. I also know that I am very important in his life and can help him. I know that he greatly appreciates me. Although a lifer, it is always possible that he will be paroled and, when older, we can live together as husband and wife. He was convicted of first-degree murder, so I realize that may never happen. I know all about his case and support him. He knows he made a horrible mistake that he, and I, must live with.

I never did ask her for details about the crime he was in prison for. "We are both very happy in our relationship and that is what is all important," she exclaimed. I do not know if a newspaper story developed from our conversation. She just wanted to meet me because her husband found our conversations very helpful in helping him adjust to prison life.

June 7, 2023. American Slavery Was Complex

No compassionate person condones selling human beings at slave auctions, nor the beating of humans who did not work as hard as their master wanted. Slavery is an unmitigated evil. Conversely, today anyone and everyone who fought for the Confederacy is condemned by many. One example is the Confederate Soldiers Monument in Durham, North Carolina; and the Screven County Confederate Dead Monument in Sylvania, Georgia, were removed. Statues of West Point graduate Robert Lee and others were torn down. Buildings named after Confederate leaders are renamed, and paintings that appear to support the South are painted over. Thomas Jefferson is condemned because he was a slave owner, as were many others of our country's leaders. Slavery and the civil war, though, is far more complex than the media present.

For example, during the civil war

> thousands of African Americans served faithfully with distinction in the armies and navies of the Confederacy. From the moment the first shots were fired on Fort Sumter, African Americans in the South rallied in defense of their country. Blacks across the country were eager to fight the enemies of their homeland. …The Confederacy officially allowed the enlistment of free blacks at a time when the North still barred African Americans from military service.[1]

Some slaves served alongside their masters. A slave named Tomas Jackson was General Robert E. Lee's "right hand man" and top lieutenant. He was mortally wounded in the May 1863 battle of Chancellorsville and honored for serving with distinction giving his life for his country.

Furthermore,

> Four million African Americans all across the South—from the Atlantic coast to the Rio Grande in Texas—supported the Confederate war machine and the fledgling nation during its life and death struggle. Their labors in the fields, railroads yards, factories, wharves, sweatshops, arsenals, and hospitals of the South fueled the rebel war effort.[2]

---

1 Phillip Tucker, *From Auction Block to Glory: The African American Experience*, (University of Wisconsin Press: Madison, WI, 1998), 72.

2 Tucker, *From Auction Block to Glory*, 72–80.

Furthermore, as the book *Black Slave Owners: Free Black Slave Masters in South Carolina, 1790–1860* documented, William Ellison Jr. (1790–1861) was a former African-American slave who became a major plantation owner and one of the wealthiest property owners in the state. His over nine hundred acres of land were worked by his sixty-eight black slaves, the largest of the 171 black slaveholders in South Carolina.

After Lincoln issued the emancipation proclamation, the North expected the civil war would be over in a few months. They expected the slaves to flee their masters *en masse*, but relatively few did. In spite of their sometimes-hard life, they loved their country as much as anyone else. This is why the movement to take Blacks to Africa utterly failed. "We are Americans. This is our county, not Arica. We were born in America and will die in America," was the dominant sentiment. The support of Blacks "for their country" caused the civil war to drag on for four long years, costing 620 thousand American lives, more than all wars Americans fought in combined. Surveys of slaves found 72 percent had very positive feelings for their masters, more than modern workers have for their boss today. Although many well-documented stories of slave masters abusing their slaves exist, slavery was much more complex than the abuses. Most well-known are the sexual abuses of female slaves, but also many cases of genuine respect between them. Like many enslaved women, Sally Hemings (1773–1835) gave birth to at least six children that were fathered by her owner, all of which were eventually freed as also was Sally.

June 14, 2023. A Visit from *60 Minutes*

As a widely published author, I often have contacts with the mass media. One summer, a producer for *60 Minutes* called me about a story they were then working on. After a long conversation, the producer and his assistant decided to fly from New York to Toledo, then rent a car to my home in Montpelier, Ohio, for an in-depth interview. We had a long conversation, and, in the end, I am confident that I learned more from them than they learned from me. They, at least a decade ago, checked and rechecked the facts related to the story they were working on. I not only conveyed to them what I knew about the case but supplied them with several names to support my claims and conclusions. I found out later that they carefully checked my information with those persons that I helped them to locate. They also, from the names I gave them, obtained other sources to confirm the information given them. They called several times later to ensure the information they had was correct. I was very impressed with their care in making certain that a fair and balanced story would result, which aired later that month. Unfortunately, it appears that this care is not always followed today, especially when it comes to politics. Modern mainstream media has lost a great deal of their past credibility due to their goal to actually *make* the news instead of just objectively *reporting* the news. And, due to its decided left slant and their goal to be politically correct in harmony with the woke agenda popular today, many journalists are not always fully honest, or they leave out important balancing information (i.e., not reporting the *whole* truth). This is why the media is less creditable today than it once was. Another factor is a major source of news today are the many excellent podcasts freely available on the internet. You can, one pundit once said, "fool some of the people all of the time and all of the people some of the time, but you cannot fool all of the people all of the time." (source unknown)

June 21, 2023. Honoring My Father for Father's Day

My father, Ernest Rudolph Bergman, was born in 1917 and died in 1998 at age eighty-one. I know very little about his life, something I should have learned about when he was alive. To avoid regret, all readers who still have their father should learn about the details of their life from him…before it's too late. Ideally, do a memory book, as my wife did with her family, the Haldimans, where each member writes a few pages about their life. We made copies, and each of our families got one.

My father was the third child of John and Mary Matilda (Maria) Bergman, both born in Finland. Their first two children were twins, and only one survived, Esther. John, a laborer, died around 1919 from pneumonia. My grandmother, uneducated and English-illiterate, struggled financially her entire life after her husband died. Unable to care for her two children, they were farmed out to various relatives. As a result, my father never had the security of two parents or a stable place to call home. As a benefit, though, he was able to travel to, and live in, several states, including New York, Minnesota, Michigan, and California.

Soon after arriving in Detroit, my father married my mother in 1943. Dad was in the US Navy then, where he served on an aircraft carrier from 1943 to 1944. My father, determined to improve himself after he married my mother, earned a BS degree in Mechanical Engineering from Wayne State University in Detroit. As I was growing up, I remember he was always involved in schoolwork, a new invention, or starting a new business. After he graduated from Wayne State, he was hired as an engineer at the Ford Motor Car Company. He learned he did not like working for someone else, so soon started several businesses. He would rather work twelve hours a day in his own business than eight hours a day for someone else. And it turned out that he often worked more than twelve hours a day. His hard work ethos greatly influenced the careers of both my two brothers and me.

His love of science also strongly influenced me. Our basement was cluttered with science books, chemicals, machinery (such as a milling machine), and scientific paraphernalia. Dad would often show me the purpose of some instrument and explain the physics behind its use. He designed a variety of science-teaching tools—several with his lifelong friend, Ralph Herring of Detroit. Dad earned several patents for his inventions: one for a geothermal heating system and an innovative stove heat exchanger (US patent 4,250,864; filed May 31, 1979).

In the early 1950s, Dad drew a 4-by-8-foot periodic table of the chemical elements by hand, using ink and drafting tools. He then silk-screened these charts and sold them to colleges and universities throughout North America. He also produced a smaller 3-by-5–foot, silk-screened, wall-size chart and an 8½-by-11–inch, offset-printed, notebook-size version. College bookstores throughout the United States sold many thousands of his charts to students until his copyright expired. Imitators then rapidly sprang up, producing similar charts out of plastic-coated paper, at a much lower price, putting my father's company out of business.

Every chemistry classroom in the country now has a 4-by-8–foot periodic table prominently displayed in the front of the room. As a chemistry graduate student at Miami University in Oxford, Ohio, in the 1990s, I saw one of his large wall charts, tattered from decades of use, still hanging on the wall! I felt very proud of my father then.

Dad also bought me a chemistry set and an atomic energy kit with a scintillator that picked up alpha particles which could be seen in the small scope when one's eyes were adjusted to the dark. When in junior high school, I wanted a microscope. Dad convinced me to buy a good used one instead of a new, inexpensive model for kids that I first had in mind. He found a reconditioned medical Bausch & Lomb® microscope at Wayne State University. It cost me $125, and a half century later I still use it. I spent years examining everything I could find that fit on a glass slide. It turned out I would spend years using microscopes in my graduate work at medical school and when teaching college.

Dad often took me to the Engineering Society of Detroit meetings to watch science films and lectures. We had long discussions about science, especially physics and chemistry, giving me a heads-up in this area that enabled me to do well in my science classes. In short, he had a profound influence on me for which I am grateful even to this day. The bottom line: *Learn as much as possible about your father while you still can.*

June 28, 2023. The Tragic Story of Deborah Kallikak

When Deborah was about seventeen years old, a new custodian was hired to work where she was institutionalized, The New Jersey Home for the Education and Care of Feeble-minded. One day an order came to fix the plumbing in her room. Deborah showed the young man named Willie the problem. She then watched him work to fix it. After a few polite introductions, after this meeting they noticed each other as they went about their daily activities at the institution. Soon they were taking long walks together and discovered they had a lot in common. Willie, a young man about age twenty-two, was a very talented wood carver. He enjoyed making furniture and knick-knacks from wood. She was well-known around the institution for her culinary, embroidery, basketry, and carpentry skills. Her favorite activity was reading, especially romance novels and historical fiction.

About this time, Willie gave her a framed photograph of himself to put in her room. The other residents commented they have never seen her so happy. Then, the administration learned about the couple and told Deborah, "You are a moron (this was once a scientific classification of an IQ from 51 to 70) and we cannot have any more degenerates like you. Willie was let go, so you won't be seeing him again." She then took the picture of Willie out of the frame and tore it up in small pieces in front of Deborah. Deborah responded, almost hysterically, "You could at least let me have the one thing I had to remember Willie by!" To which the administrator said, "You will have to forget him, and the sooner the better. You are feebleminded and should never have children. We have to stop the spread of your kind." Deborah later retrieved the picture fragments, taped them together, and stored them in a secret compartment she built into one of her tables.

Friends said she was never the same after Willie was out of her life but did the best she could to adjust. In fact, both Deborah and Willie had low IQs. The difference was she was an inmate and he worked for the institution. Her family story, titled *The Kallikak Family,* published in 1912 became a best-seller. Later, the US Supreme Court approved preventing "feebleminded" persons like Deborah from propagating by sterilizing them, writing, "Three generations of imbeciles are enough." Deborah died in 1978 at the age of eighty-nine. It was a tragic story, only one small part of the eugenics movement which resulted in over sixty thousand women sterilized in the US alone. This was one of the many sad fruits of the eugenics movement birthed by Charles Darwin and his cousin, Francis Galton, that eventually produced the Holocaust in Nazi Germany.

"Deborah Kallikak," born Emma Wolverton (1889–1978) reading, her favorite activity, with her best friend, her cat.

July 5, 2023. The Tragic Story of Bertha and Clarence with a Happy Ending

When working for the court as a research psychologist, I would often be asked about memorable cases I was involved with. One I will never forget was the story of Bertha and Clarence. Clarence was a very successful businessman with a reputation of being somewhat ruthless. As a very handsome, very wealthy man, he had the pick of beautiful women. He finally married at age thirty-two to Bertha, an aspiring movie star who never progressed beyond bit parts in grade-B movies. Bertha was five years younger than Clarence. The marriage did not start off well and got worse as time went on. Finally, after five very unhappy years, Bertha filed for divorce. Clarence consulted his friend and attorney, Raymond Johns, whom Clarence had worked with for over a decade. "She will attempt to take you to the cleaners," Raymond warned Clarence, "unless we confront her in court for what she is, a gold digger." In court, Raymond, as he said he would, aggressively confronted her: "Why do you have the gall to think, after less than five years of marriage, you deserve half of this man's income that he has been earning since high school?"

After what Clarence felt was like fifteen minutes of similar aggressive questioning, Clarence stood up and said, "Could I have a word with the judge?" After Raymond objected, the judge said, "Yes, I need to hear what he has to say." Clarence then said to the judge, "I cannot, and will not, allow this haranguing of my wife (they were still married then). I love her and do not want to see her being pummeled like this. We are two very different people and, for her sake, we should not be married. I want what is best for her. If she gives me a list of what she wants from our home and savings, I will give her everything she asks for." After this speech, over Raymond's objections, the judge formalized his proposal. It turned out what she asked for was less than what lawyer Raymond determined she would get from the divorce. It also turned out that she never forgot Raymond's kindness for her in court.

Bertha remarried less than a year after the divorce was final. After what friends described was a perfect twenty-four-year marriage, her husband, who was seven years older than her, died of a massive heart attack. Clarence attended the funeral, and he and Bertha soon became reacquainted. Clarence had never remarried, was in his seventies now, and in poor health. His lifelong, high-stress personality had left him with decades-long high blood pressure, and he was also diabetic. Then he had a heart attack. After several long phone calls and visits, Bertha made it clear to him that she was going to move in to help him. "You have six bedrooms, so have plenty of room for me," she told him. As a nurse, she wanted to care for him; and, given his poor health, he realized that he needed the care she offered. Bertha and Clarence soon remarried. They lived a simple life and adopted an adorable dog, which they walked in the local park several times a day. They often went to concerts and movies and especially spent time reading. Clarence began writing for business magazines and even began drafting his autobiography. His wife lovingly served as his supportive critic and Clarence ended up an award-winning writer. They also became involved in a Bible church and Clarence, a Jew, learned about the most famous Jew that ever lived, Yeshua, who was born in Bethlehem. As a Hebrew school graduate, Clarence taught Sunday school, and they were otherwise very involved in their church. They made it a point to invite several people to their home for conversation once a week. Several times a year missionaries stayed in their large home.

Bertha took care of Clarence until he died seventeen years later, living far longer than his high-paid doctors predicted. They both agreed that their seventeen years together were the best years of their lives. The heart attack turned out to be a blessing. The doctors stated that the reason he lived so long was the excellent care he received from Bertha. When Bertha died a few years later, on their tombstone was written, "Here lies Bertha and Clarence Cohen. May they be together for eternity."

July 25, 2023. How Race Preferences Damage Higher Education

Anyone who has been employed recently as an academic is aware of a dangerous trend: the abandonment of meritocracy. Meritocracy, hiring and promotion on the basis of merit, was the norm for over a century. Although it made the United States the most prosperous country in the world, it is now under aggressive attack by the equity crowd. Affirmative action has resulted in problems, especially at top-flight universities where academically weaker, minority students compete with academically much stronger White and Asian students. In the end, this harms both Black and Hispanic students. It would be better if they graduated at the top of the class at an average university than at the bottom of the class at an Ivy League college.

The well-known case of Allan Bakke illustrates a major concern with affirmative action. By the 1970s, affirmative action was established policy at many colleges. In response, the University of California-Davis devised an affirmative action plan for its medical school. The plan called for 84 percent of openings to be filled according to traditional academic qualifications, while 16 percent were set aside for "disadvantaged" applicants, mostly racial minorities. One White applicant, Allan Bakke, was rejected twice under this plan. His undergraduate GPA was 3.44 while the disadvantaged track science average GPA was 2.62. In contrast to the "disadvantaged" track, which was in the 35th percentile, Bakke's MCAT score for science was in the 97th percentile. Bakke clearly performed better than almost every minority hopeful.

Bakke realized that this was an example of the harm caused by "equity" goals, coupled with the rejection of merit-based consideration. Bakke sued, alleging that he was the victim of racial discrimination. Bakke, the son of a mail carrier and school teacher, served in Vietnam as a medic, and volunteered at local emergency rooms. His life goal was to become a doctor. Bakke prevailed in the lower courts, so U.C.-Davis appealed to the California Supreme Court. In 1976 the California high court decided 6-to-1 in favor of Bakke. Judge Stanley Mosk wrote the decision in favor of Bakke and against the university. He reasoned that, to rule in favor of affirmative action "would represent a retreat in the struggle to assure that each man and woman shall be judged based on individual merit alone." As a result of his written decision, Judge Mosk became the subject of denunciations, student protesters screaming outside his office window, and mobs condemning him.

U.C.-Davis appealed to the US Supreme Court. In 1978 the four conservative justices affirmed the lower court's ruling, and four liberal judges upheld the university's racial favoritism that permitted discrimination against White applicants. Justice Louis Powell Jr. found the University of California-Davis affirmative action policy unconstitutional. Consequently, the 4-to-5 decision admitted Bakke into medical school.

In 2003 the Supreme Court again took up the affirmative action issue. Justice O'Connor wrote for the majority upholding affirmative action. Chief Justice Rehnquist noted in his dissent that the Civil Rights Act of 1964 made quotas illegal. Justice Harry Blackmun wrote that this decision was a "regrettable but necessary stage of 'transitional inequality,'" hoping that it would end "within a decade at the most." In 2003, Justice O'Connor, wrote that she hoped the policy would end within twenty-five years. It actually ended only a few days ago with the Supreme Court ruling that discrimination based on race is unconstitutional. Predictably, the media blasted the Supreme Court for what they called this racist ruling.

Columbia University professor Nicholas Lemann sought to bolster the importance of affirmative action by contrasting the careers of the two doctors: Allan Bakke, who was originally denied admission to University of California Medical School, and Patrick Chavis, a Black applicant, who, though he scored much lower on objective examinations and received lower grades, was admitted through its disadvantaged program. Chavis, the son of a single mother, grew up poor but pressed forward. After graduation from medical school, Chavis served the poor Black community of Compton. By contrast, the White Bakke became an anesthetist working in a White area of the Middle West. Dr. Chavis, through affirmative action admission to medical school, provided a public service to the community beyond being another doctor. He paid back to the community in a way Bakke did not. Thus, Lemann argued, affirmative action is necessary for the good of everyone.

However, the story does not end well. On June 19, 1997, the Medical Board of California suspended Chavis's license to practice medicine after documenting he was unable to perform some of the most basic medical duties and was guilty of gross negligence and incompetence when treating patients—evidently some died due to his incompetence. The poster boy of affirmative action became the poster boy against affirmative action. Ironically, the Chavis story failed to be reported by most major media outlets. Unquestionably, in critical areas like medicine and in professions like airline pilots, merit *must* be the *only* criteria used to train and employ.

July 19, 2023. How Much Do Students Learn in College?

Free college and loan forgiveness are major planks of Biden's New Deal. The problem is far too many people now go to college that have no business attending. Many survive because, if a professor flunks too many students, he/she will be invited for a chat with the Dean. Survival for a professor often means requiring minimal standards. Three exams and a short paper is common. Requiring significantly more work may also merit a visit to the Dean's office. Students are paying customers, and the college needs to retain as many students as possible to pay for the recent ballooning of administration costs, such as the high-paid diversity and affirmative action deans.

The big question is: how much learning now days goes on in the hallowed halls of academia? Today most young persons aspire to go to college, but few ask the fundamental question posed by one study of 2,300 undergraduates by Richard Arum and Josipa Roksa in their book titled, *Academically Adrift: Limited Learning on College Campuses.* The question they researched was "how much are undergraduates learning once they get into college?" For a large proportion of students, the Arum and Roksa research found the answer was a definitive not much. Their extensive research used the survey responses, transcript data, and the *Collegiate Learning Assessment*, a standardized test administered to students in their first semester of college, which they then retake at the end of their second year.

Their analysis of a representative sample of twenty-four colleges, found fully 45 percent of the students surveyed demonstrated no significant improvement in basic academic skills—critical thinking, complex reasoning, and writing skills—during their first two years of college. And 36 percent showed very little improvement after four years of college. Significant learning was found *only* in their major area of study, presumably because their main interest was in that area, as was much of their coursework. Part of the problem was the lack of rigor required now in college. Even in their major, half of the students did not take a single course requiring a total of over nineteen pages of writing, and one-third did not take a single class requiring over thirty-nine pages of reading a week.

Arum and Roksa note that the results were not a surprise for many faculty and administrators—instead, they expected these results from a student body distracted by sports, dating, partying, or working outside jobs, and an institutional culture that puts learning close to the bottom of their priority list.

When I was a professor at Bowling Green State University, one of my Black students missed close to half of my classes. When I asked why, he said he had football practice. When I asked why he didn't take classes at the time when he did not have practice, he said he was there to play football and that had to be his priority. A few days later, I received a phone call from the coach. He explained my student was a star player and, he added, he needed to maintain a certain honor-point average to stay on the team. Furthermore, I needed to help him achieve that goal. He was very polite but made it clear it would not help my career at BGSU to give him a poor grade. I got the point and gave him an undeserved B. To survive as a faculty, a professor has to learn to deal with contingencies such as this. After all, we all know sports are a critical part of college because they are a major source of income. Sports are also a major means of attracting students.

July 26, 2023. The Truth About COVID Vaccination Surfacing

During the COVID epidemic, I became aware of three athletic young men who, within close to a week of receiving the COVID shot, all died of heart failure. This could be due to chance, but it made me wonder. One healthy, young, twenty-eight-year-old man was the son of a physician. The father related to me that his son's death was caused by myocarditis related to the COVID vaccine that he had just gotten a week before. Since then, I have learned of various claims by friends claiming the same thing happened in their family. A new study lent evidence to my suspicions. The study found, of 325 autopsies they reviewed, 240 deaths, or 74 percent, were independently adjudicated as "directly due to or significantly contributed to by COVID-19 vaccination." The autopsies showed the most-affected organ system in COVID-19 vaccine-associated death was the cardiovascular system. The rate was 53 percent, followed by the hematological system, 17 percent, the respiratory system, 8 percent, and multiple-organ systems, 7 percent. The average time from vaccination to death was 14.3 days.

The lead author, internist, cardiologist, and epidemiologist Dr. Peter McCullough, noted, "The striking cases were of people who were perfectly healthy and had no other medical problems. The only new thing in their life was the vaccine, and they died with an obvious syndrome like a blood clot or heart damage—myocarditis."

The study was soon removed by the journal that had originally published it. According to Dr. Peter A. McCullough, MD, MPH, the authors were not given a valid explanation for how their conclusions failed to meet their study standards. Co-author, senior epidemiology research scientist at Yale University, Dr. Harvey Risch, stated that he believes the paper was censored by *Lancet*'s publisher, Elsevier. Dr. McCullough noted that the project was approved through the University of Michigan's School of Public Health, and the team used the standard scientific evaluation methodology called the *Preferred Reporting Items for Systematic Reviews and Meta-Analyses*. They searched through hundreds of papers to identify forty-four cases that met the research criteria.

Dr. McCullough was not a novice researcher. He has published more than one thousand scientific articles that were cited by 660 journals. The study's co-authors included top pathologist Dr. Roger Hodkinson, former chairman of the Royal College of Physicians and Surgeons of Canada's examination committee in pathology, and Dr. Paul Alexander, of the US Department of Health and Human Services. Dr. McCullough said that before its removal, the study had hundreds of views. Fortunately, it is now on the Zenodo preprint server (https://zenodo.org/record/8120771) and has had almost seventy-seven thousand views and sixty-three thousand downloads.

Another study by Dr. McCullough and molecular biologist Dr. Jessica analyzed data from the Vaccine Adverse Event Reporting System (VAERS) and found myocarditis spiked in teenagers after COVID-19 vaccination. McCullough's co-researchers included Nicolas Hulscher, BS; Paul E. Alexander, PhD; Richard Amerling, MD; Heather Gessling, MD; Roger Hodkinson, MD; William Makis, MD; Harvey A. Risch, MD, PhD; and Mark Trozzi, MD. Vaccine papers get special attention because some people do not want to have the safety data presented because it may discourage people who need the vaccine from getting it. I believe that sooner or later the facts about this concern will be public.

August 2,2023. From Deborah Kallikak to the Holocaust

My earlier column on Deborah Kallikak brought several responses, mostly asking how a multitalented girl could ever be judged as feeble-minded. She was judged feeble-minded by the psychologists using tests which have now been shown to be very problematic. The story of Deborah's family, titled *The Kallikak Family*, written by Harvard-trained biologist Charles Davenport and Ohio State University professor Henry Goddard, was soon retold in hundreds of books. One of the worst examples was in the textbook used by John Scopes titled *A Civic Biology* by George William Hunter (1863–1948). This textbook, which openly taught racism, contained an entire chapter on eugenics based on the Kallikak family. For nearly a decade, Hunter's book was the most widely used high school science textbook in America. It was endorsed by many distinguished professors, including those at elite universities such as Brown (Providence, Rhode Island) and Columbia (New York, New York).

Hunter's *Civic Biology* text describes the Kallikak study in glowing terms as definitive proof of the inheritance of feeble-mindedness, alcoholism, immorality, and criminality. Hunter proposed in his text that, to solve most social problems, all we had to do was identify the genetic human carriers of certain maladies such as feeble-mindedness, then sterilize them to ensure that these traits were eventually eradicated from humanity. As late as 1955, one leading high school biology textbook uncritically endorsed the claim that the feeble-minded Deborah Kallikak clan had caused enormous harm to society.

> Between 1907 and 1963, at least 60,000 persons were sterilized in the United States for eugenic reasons, the majority being women. To silence the opposition against eugenics from the churches that taught all humans were children of Adam and Eve, and no races were therefore inferior, the eugenicists brought a case to the Supreme Court. The Court sided with the eugenicists. The highly respected Supreme Court Justice Oliver Wendell Holmes ruled because heredity plays an important part in the transmission of insanity, imbecility, …it is better for all the world, if instead of waiting to execute degenerate offspring for crime, or to let them starve for their imbecility, society can prevent those who are manifestly unfit from continuing their kind. The principle that sustains compulsory vaccination is broad enough to cover cutting the fallopian tubes. Three generations of imbeciles are enough.[1]

---

1 US Supreme Court Case *Buck v. Bell*, 274 U.S. 200 (1927), 206–207.

The Deborah *Kallikak Family* story was enormously important for the eugenics movement, not only in America, but also in Nazi Germany. Hitler learned about the Kallikak Family study when he was imprisoned in 1924 for his part in the Nazi's attempt to overthrow the government by force. The year Hitler assumed power in Germany, 1933, a German language edition of *The Kallikak Family,* translated by Karl Wilker, was published. In his introduction, Wilker made it clear how important the Kallikak Family research was in Nazi Germany's adoption of eugenic programs. The Nazis even used the book's conclusions as a teaching tool in German schools. The result of the German indoctrination program was the Nazi government eventually murdered over two hundred thousand persons they judged either feeble-minded or part of what the Nazis regarded as an inferior race.

We now know *The Kallikak Family* book was a grossly distorted account based on the conviction that Darwinian eugenics could improve society. Deborah, who was not educated in regular schools, may not have done well on the Stanford-Binet IQ test, but she was nevertheless a very talented woman who mastered many skills, including cooking, embroidery, basketry, and woodworking. She also played the cornet beautifully and was a talented actress, playing the star roles in the performances put on by the institution (i.e., New Jersey's Vineland Training School). Deborah also helped to care for the children of the institution's employees. The children absolutely adored her, some of whom sent letters to her for the rest of her life.

In the end, the eugenics movement led to the Holocaust and the murder of twelve million people judged inferior by the leading professors and doctors in the most educated nation on Earth, Germany. The indoctrination into Darwinism that occurred in Nazi Germany by the educated elite still plagues the world today. No longer is the indoctrination focused on Darwinian racism, but on the total Darwinian evolutionary worldview.

This worldview philosophy has replaced theism with functional atheism and an intolerance for the theistic worldview and its values. Both Darwinian racism and Darwinian evolutionism are myths that have caused an enormous amount of suffering. As Professor Søren Løvtrup, when chairman of the Swedish Developmental Biologists, has said in his book *Darwinism: The Refutation of a Myth,* "I believe that one day the Darwinian myth will be ranked the greatest deceit in the history of science. When this happens, many people will pose the question: how did this ever happen?"[2]

---

2   Søren Løvtrup, *Darwinism: The Refutation of a Myth,* (Springer, 1987), 422.

Deborah Kallikak

August 9, 2023. Are Human Males and Females Different Genders?

When a child comes into the world, the first thing noted is their sex. Is it a boy or a girl? For the rest of their life the most prominent fact about most people is their sex. Sports, bathrooms, friends, medical charts, and much of their life is segregated by sex. Every society for the last six thousand years has separated male and female roles and responsibilities. Males and females had very different places in life and society, and their families expected them to conform to these roles. The specifics varied, but generally men focused on hunting, farming, and, in general, working outdoors at hard-labor tasks such as construction. Women's roles included bearing and raising children, sewing, making clothes, and the basic housekeeping tasks. Marriage between a man and a woman was the norm in most every society in history.

Nonetheless, today, more so than any other time in history, people are questioning if the human sexes are really very different. Sexual differences have been studied even before Aristotle walked the earth in ancient Greece. The differences have been studied in many research areas including psychology, sociology, anatomy, biochemistry, cell biology, physiology, histology, and all areas of medicine from disease to immunology. *The findings were very clear.* Not in one single trait are the averages of males and females identical. Females, *on average*, ranked higher than males, or males, *on average*, ranked higher than females. Individual females sometimes score higher than the average male, and individual males sometimes score higher than the average female on other traits.

Furthermore, to ignore the differences between males and females can be dangerous. One of many examples that illustrates this fact was the medication Zolpidem (used to treat insomnia), sold widely as Ambien, which I reported on in this column on January 25, 2023. I then noted that for years, only males were tested to determine proper drug dosage. It was then learned that a much higher rate of women taking Ambien were too sleepy to drive safely the next morning. Research found that, because women metabolized the drug differently than males, women got twice the proper dose. The result was a rash of traffic accidents. Women who used Ambien had a 61 percent higher probability of a crash over five years compared to nonusers. A major reason for the variance was due to male and female hormone differences. Another example is women have lower concentrations of alcohol dehydrogenase, the enzyme that breaks down ethanol. Thus, they became inebriated much sooner than males because it takes them *longer* to breakdown the alcohol. For this reason, its toxic effects are greater.

The biological difference between males and females is so great that every somatic cell in the body, in all from thirty-seven trillion to ten thousand trillion, depending on the weight of the person, is different (XY for males, XX for females).

Although red blood cells become enucleated (expel their nucleus to give more room to do their job in the body, i.e. carry oxygen) all other cells, including bone cells, retain their nucleus until the person dies. Even in death, sexual differences remain. When a human skeleton is found, the first step in identifying the body is to determine the sex. The sex is often obvious from the bone structure, but if all else fails, chromosomal analysis, and even DNA, can be used. The next step is to determine who the victim was, and why did he/she die. Murder? Suicide? Accident?

The Judeo-Christian scriptures are very clear about male/female differences. Humans were created male and female, and the female was created to be a compliment for the male. Likewise, the male was created to be a compliment for the female. As Genesis 2:18, 21–24 reads:

> *The Lord God said, "It is not good for the man to be alone. I will make a helper suitable for him." ...So God caused the man to fall into a deep sleep; and while he was sleeping, [from his side] God made a woman, ...and he brought her to the man. The man said, "...she shall be called 'woman,' for she was taken out of man." That is why a man leaves his father and mother and is united to his wife, and they become one flesh* [emotionally, intellectually, financially mentally, spiritually, and psychologically].

August 16, 2023. Turning Soil into Humans

Humans require about fifty-two different elements to survive. Fully 99 percent of our body is composed of only six elements: oxygen, hydrogen, nitrogen, carbon, calcium, and phosphorus. Another five elements namely, sulfur, potassium, sodium, chlorine, and magnesium, make up about 0.85 percent of the remaining mass. The trace elements: chromium, copper, gold, iron, fluorine, zinc, and thirty-five others make up only 0.15 percent of the human body. Nevertheless, although only small amounts are required, these trace elements are critical for life. Zinc alone is required by over three hundred enzymes. All of these chemicals and elements are found in the soil. We are thus, ultimately, made of dirt, which normally contains all fifty-two elements required for life. Plants require soil to obtain the elements they need for life and growth, and we then eat the plants to obtain the elements we require (and/or we eat the animals, such as cows, which eat the plants).

Chemists have been able to synthesize in the laboratory the vitamins, hormones, and antibiotics, plus all twenty amino acids that we require in addition to the thousands of proteins not found in our natural environment. Although scientists can produce these key parts of the human body, they are not even close to producing an entire body of any life-form, ranging from bacteria to man, from nonliving elements. And even if scientists could produce an entire mouse or human body, it would not be *alive*. We are chemical machines but are not alive until we are given *the breath of life*. This science confirms the Bible teaching that "the LORD God formed the man from the dust of the ground and breathed into his nostrils the breath of life, and the man became a living being" (Genesis 2:7). To reinforce this, the word "human" is derived from the Latin word "*humus*," meaning earth, soil, or ground.

Scientists have, however, attempted to grow human organs in other mammals, such as pigs, by introducing human stem cells into early-stage animal embryos. Human pluripotent (self-renewing) stem cells can become part of ungulate embryos (ungulates primarily consist of large mammals with hooves), but this process is very inefficient. Pluripotent cells can give rise to several different cell types by developing into either of the three primary groups of body cells: the ectoderm, the mesoderm, or the endoderm. Even if this technique is someday successful, it does not create *life* but rather modifies existing life.

Cells have been made by combining components of *Mycoplasma* bacteria with a chemically synthesized genome that can grow and divide into cells of uniform shape and size, similar to natural bacterial cells. Again, this is not the creation of life, but only the modifying of pre-existing life. This is the type of work I did when employed at the Medical College of Ohio. We synthesized DNA and used gain-of-function technology to splice the DNA we synthesized into Lambda virus which were then used to infect various types of living cells. The result of this process was that we were able to modify the DNA in living cells. Again, this technique only modifies living cells. It does not create life from nonlife but uses laboratory-constructed DNA to modify already-existing life.

The *simplest* known living organism is the *Carsonella ruddii* bacterium that has over 159,662 DNA base pairs which involve several trillion properly assembled molecules. This example illustrates the fact that the simplest known living organisms are enormously complex. Yet evolutionists claim that life developed from, as Darwin and his followers spectated, molecules that self-assembled in a warm little pond added by lightning to provide energy.

Science can grow some body parts in the laboratory but has not been able to make nonliving chemicals *alive* in the sense that animals are alive, in spite of thousands of scientists working for over five decades attempting to do so. Craig Venter created synthetic "minimal" cells by removing genes from living cells. The genome in each modified cell contained just 473 key genes thought to be essential for life. The cells were able to grow and divide on agar medium to produce clusters of cells called colonies. But their daughter cells had bizarre shapes and sizes. They had removed all the genome DNA that they thought were not essential for growth. But the so-called not essential parts they removed were, in-fact, required.

Scientists never have, and I believe they never will, make nonliving chemicals alive animals (including mammals, reptiles, amphibians, and birds). They are alive only because life can give life. The best example of the fact that only life gives life is the birth process. And the first life-giver was God from Whom all life existing today has come (John 1:4). No other possibility exists.

August 23, 2023. Censoring the G-Word from Science

One of the requirements of a professor is to review new curriculum material for its appropriateness for classroom use. Part of this requirement involved watching films on science and current event topics that may be appropriate. I soon got into the habit of watching hundreds of DVDs. After I retired, I continued to watch DVDs of interest. I now have watched several thousand of the DVDs in my library, mostly on science and history. I have noted one word that, with one exception, was never mentioned, namely "God." The one mention was in a Neil deGrasse Tyson DVD, which was very negative about theism and persons who believe in God.

Even in a context that would seem to require the mention of God, the word and concept was ignored. For example, cosmologist professor Bran Green produced a video about the origin of our universe in which he mentioned that one cosmology difficulty was, "Why is our Earth the right size, the proper location from the Sun, not too close or too far away, to support life?" He added our moon was the right size and distance from the Earth, which is also necessary to support life. Other requirements for life included the Earth's surface being 70 percent water.

After mentioning several other life-friendly coincidences, Professor Greene noted that no other planet in our solar system, nor any one of the over five hundred planets discovered in other solar systems, can brag about being able to support life. This fact is one of the most well-known means of supporting the existence of an intelligent Creator God. God made the Earth specifically to support life and no other planet can support life (Isa. 45:18). Greene never mentioned this option but rather noted that the only explanation for the existence of our privileged planet was there must be millions of other universes, and we happen to live in the one that has a solar system which contains a planet that can support life. The problem with this explanation, which he ignored, is that absolutely no evidence exists for universes other than our own. This belief, called the multiverse, has been bandied about for some time, and as of yet no one has been able to even postulate how this theoretical multiverse could be documented.

Another DVD, produced by Professor Brian Cox, asks, "Why are we here? Where did we come from? What is our future?" The Judeo-Christian-Muslim faiths answer these questions by noting that God created us, and we are here to carry out God's purpose for life on Earth. And, lastly, God has a plan for us in the future, including everlasting life in paradise. Cox related the evolutionary view, namely that we evolved due to time, chance, the accumulation of genetic mutations (genetic errors), and natural selection (that fitter life-forms are more likely to survive). Our sun will eventually burn out, the solar system will be destroyed, and all life everywhere will cease to exist. The one hundred billion galaxies that contain many hundreds of billions of stars will all burn out and, eventually, the entire universe will deteriorate due to entropy. In the end, all atoms and molecules will decay, and all that will exist in the entire universe will be photons. And for all eternity, no life will ever exist anywhere. The now empty universe will be empty for all eternity.

Frankly, this end, which Professor Cox eloquently described, is depressing. He never mentioned the belief of billions of Christians, Muslims, and Jews, that God teaches an outcome quite different than the morose predictions of secular atheistic scientists. Likewise, this same atheistic theme was presented in the thousands of science films I have watched, although more tactfully and less blunt. This includes in films that eloquently presented the wonders of our physical world in glorious detail backed by enchanting music. They all display in color our enchanting world which is why I watch one of these enlightening science DVDs most every evening although they never mention God.

August 30, 2023. World War II: The War That Never Should Have Happened

In college I had an opportunity to earn six of my history credits by signing up for a three-month European Study Tour. Besides listening to lectures as we traveled from city to city on the train, a paper on some aspect of the tour was required. I decided to interview persons to answer the question as to why Christianity had lost most of its adherents after the war. For example, post-war church attendance has shrunk to under 30 percent in Germany. In most every major city we visited, I was able to make contacts with persons I knew from my correspondence. From them I was able to enjoy a personal tour of the city and visits to pubs where I could interview persons involved in World War II, mostly local citizens.

One very useful interview was with a man in the Netherlands. He related that, between May 10 and 14 of 1940, the German Luftwaffe leveled the beautiful historical city of Rotterdam, making it clear that every Dutch city would be obliterated unless the country unconditionally surrendered. Over 1,150 people were killed and eighty-five thousand more were left homeless. If the Dutch command did not surrender, Oberkommando der Luftwaffe (Upper Command of the Air Force) threatened next to destroy Utrecht, the fourth-largest city in the Netherlands. The Dutch surrendered in the afternoon of May 14 and signed the capitulation early the next morning.

Even though my interview occurred over twenty years after the war, the anger in his voice was striking. He lost his family, his home, most of his friends, and, although he found refuge, he saw firsthand the brutal treatment meted out to the Dutch people by the Germans. Netherlands was a neutral country during both World War I and World War II, but they were treated as if they were Germany's enemy. My informant lost his Jewish boss who lived in the same apartment building that he did. His apartment was raided at 2 AM, and he and his entire family were taken away, never to be seen again. Those arrested had no warning of the arrest, thus they could not flee and were unprepared to resist. Ironically, my informant, although a blond-haired, blue-eyed man, worked for a Jewish company and therefore was interrogated. His mother was Dutch, his father, German. They lived not far from the German border and had relatives in Germany.

During a visit to a cousin in Germany during the war, he visited several German Lutheran churches, explaining to me,

> The pastors prayed for victory in the war, eulogizing the Nazi troops who were killed by enemy soldiers, in this case Dutch and Americans. On the wall of one church I visited was a sign which stated in German "In honor

of the Brave soldiers killed by the enemy fighting for their country, Germany." From my perspective, they were the enemy, killing us Dutch.

One pastor explained, "We clergy try to stay out of politics, but Germany had a right to defend itself from its enemies. The Treaty of Versailles, which formally ended World War One, was signed on June 28, 1919. The terms required that Germany pay enormous financial reparations (132 billion gold marks, equivalent to US $442 billion), disarm, lose much of our territory, and give up all of our overseas colonies."

When I asked about the Jews, the pastor responded with Nazi propaganda, "It was because of them that we lost the war. We Germans are the superior race, and the Jews have robbed us blind."

One of the few churches that openly opposed the Nazi war was the Confessing Church, which was Dietrich Bonhoeffer's church. World War II was the deadliest military conflict in history. From seventy to eighty-five million people perished. Deaths directly caused by the war (including military and civilian fatalities) were close to fifty-six million, with an additional twenty-eight million deaths from war-related disease and famine. Civilian deaths totaled fifty-five million. Military deaths from all causes totaled twenty-five million, including the deaths of about 5 million prisoners of war.

All of the nations involved in both sides of the European Theater were Christian but ignored the teachings of the person they claimed to follow who preached,

You have heard that it was said, "You shall love your neighbor, and hate your enemy." But I tell you, love your enemies and pray for those persecuting you, to be children of your Father in heaven. For He causes His sun to rise on the evil and the good and sends rain on the righteous and the unrighteous (Matt. 5:43).

Jesus told his disciple Peter, "Put your sword back in its place because all who take up the sword will perish by the sword (Matt. 26:52–53)." "Blessed are the peacemakers, for they shall be called sons of God (Matt. 5:9)."

My conclusion from my interviews was that a major reason for the population's abandonment of Christianity was disillusionment with the churches because they did almost nothing to prevent and oppose the Nazi carnage. The tragedy was, they abandoned Christianity not because of its Christian teachings, but because the churches had abandoned Jesus' teachings. Eric Metaxas in his new best-selling book *Letter to the American Church* (with 1,883 reviews on Amazon), warns of haunting parallels between the compliant Nazi Germany churches and our churches today. Echoing Bonhoeffer's prophetic call, Metaxas exhorts his fellow Christians to learn from the face of evil in Germany. Germany, too, suffered greatly. In total, seventy-two German cities were destroyed by the allies, and German military casualties were 5.3 million plus an estimated five hundred thousand civilians killed in the Allied strategic bombing. Lastly, three hundred thousand Aryan Germans and twelve million non-Germans were systematically murdered due to the German Darwinian eugenic programs to "purify" the Aryan race. The Nazi priority was to exterminate inferior races. I document in my latest book that if they had accepted the Bible teaching that we are all descendants of Adam and Eve, thus only one human race exists, there would likely never have been a World War II.

September 6, 2023. Coping with Loss of Friends Is Hard

The loss of long-term friends has always been very difficult for me. One recent loss was especially difficult. This was the loss of Dr. Thomas Stogdill, MD. He was a very special person in my life. He was eighty-eight when he passed away on August 10 this year, so was blessed with a long and very productive life. We met after I published an article in *The Fort Wayne Journal-Gazette* in 2006 on the Bible and science. He wrote to me about my article, and we soon corresponded by email which was a godsend for both of us. We were in so many ways alike in interests.

After living out West for many years, he returned to Bluffton, Indiana, in 1986, to work at Caylor-Nickel Clinic. Much of his life was giving to others. He was instrumental in establishing the Panos Free Clinic in 1991, where he served as vice president of the board for fifteen years. He was also president of the board for the Council on Aging, a board member of the Boys & Girls Clubs of America and the Wells County Foundation, where he was chair of the Grants Committee. He was a Big Brothers/Big Sisters volunteer and was a member of the Human Rights Committee for Bi-County Services. As an active pro-life supporter, he was deeply concerned about Christian social issues.

We both were very interested in science and Christianity, especially the biological origins issue, as well as medicine. I was then doing research and teaching at the Medical College of Ohio. Thomas was also the author of two books and would also help me with my writing. As an excellent editor, he would often catch things that I missed, as well as challenge me on a few of my more esoteric ideas. He also wrote introductions and endorsements to several of my books. As a long-time subscriber to several science magazines, he was up-to-date on many aspects of science which helped to stimulate our conversations.

We both had major reservations about many evolutionary claims and reinforced each other's concerns when these issues surfaced in the scientific literature. Foremost, he realized that God revealed himself not only through His word but also his works, his creation. And one can learn a great deal about God though studying his creation just as one can learn a great deal about an artist by studying his art.

Success as a writer depends on one's editors and associates. In some ways, Tom was one of my co-authors that I worked with. There is no way I could have published sixty books in twelve languages and close to 1800 articles without Dr. Stogdill's help, as well as the assistance of many other supporters. He would also keep me updated on the success of his family members, whom he loved and of which he was very proud.

Speaking of family, on a personal note, on July 15, 1966, Tom wedded Lou Ann Carlson in Las Vegas. After over twenty years of marriage, she preceded him in death in 1987. It was very clear that he missed his wife enormously. I once asked him if, as a successful physician, he had ever considered remarrying. He ardently explained that Lou Ann was his first and only love, and nobody could ever replace her. This was typical of his dedication to others, especially his family.

Dr. Thomas Stogdill

September 13, 2023. Darwinism: A Major Cause of Christianity's Demise

A new book titled *Life After Christendom* by NASA scientist Craig Davis has attempted to explain the reasons for fall of Christianity in the West. One factor he explored was so-called "higher criticism," the scholarly trend to look for reasons to question the validity of the Bible and the existence of God. One good example of this is Julies Wellhausen (1844–1918), who conducted a "scientific study" of the Bible by applying the theory of evolution to the Bible. He believed that the Bible evolved from a lower to a higher level of complexity.

His supporters believed that he was enormously successful in his goal of reducing the credibility of the Bible and, as a professor of theology, his ideas have influenced thousands of students, both then and today. A large number of theology professors today have accepted evolution and, at some level, have consequently rejected the Adam and Eve account as historical fact. Wellhausen's critics, of which there were many, have discerned major gaps in his reasoning, but unless one is willing to explore both sides of the question, one will not discern the many problems with his reasoning. College students often learn only the one side and are rarely exposed to the many major problems with Wellhausen's views.

Wide acceptance of certain non-Christian ideas has also taken its toll on the church. To use Sweden as a typical example, even though 80 percent of Swedes are today "members" of the Church of Sweden, only 4 percent attended church weekly. Although 15 percent of the Swedish population believed in the personal God of the Bible, 17 percent believed in the Hindu idea of reincarnation. Both spiritual apathy and theological ignorance are plaguing today's church, which is one major reason for its decline.

After reviewing every plausible reason for the demise of Christendom, Davis showed that Darwinism was one of the chief reasons for the public loss of belief in Christianity and God. The decline in religious conviction in the West can be traced back to the publication of the *Origin of Species* by Charles Darwin in 1859. Before Darwin, the vast majority of persons in the West, including naturalists, were creationists. After Darwin, nonbelief has grown until, among well-educated scientists, the vast majority are functional atheists. A functional atheist often will not self-label as an atheist but, nevertheless, lives his life as if there is no God.

For example, for the past two centuries the nation of Netherlands has collected very good historical statistics on the religious beliefs of its people. In 1859, not a single person in the country's poll identified as having no religion, or of being an atheist. In 1879, the number declaring themselves as atheists was only 0.3 percent, but since then this number has made a steady increase until today the majority of Dutch list themselves as atheists.

This is understandable because the main reason most people say they believe in God is due to the wonder and beauty of the natural world, including animal life, the beauty of plants, and the complexity of design. Charles Darwin, realizing this fact, once stated that his goal was to "murder God," meaning to cause people to reject Him. To do this he had to come up with another explanation to explain the existence and design of the natural world. This "other explanation' was intentionally done by him and others in order to strategically destroy the primary reason people believe in God.

This alternative secular explanation for the origin of the creation that Darwin and his disciples promoted was evolution, often called Darwinism. Evolution of life, according to modern naturalists, works by genetic mutations producing genetic variety, then the superior varieties are supposedly preserved by natural selection, a process called "survival of the fittest." In short, evolutionists believe that *everything* evolves: life, the Earth, the stars, the sun, and even matter itself. If Darwin could visit the West today, he would be amazed at how successful he was, far beyond his wildest dreams. As Craig Davis has documented in his book, *Life After Christendom*, the propagation of the Darwinist worldview in our educational enterprises has been a leading reason why God has been driven out of Western society.

Charles Darwin age 75

September 20, 2023. Is the Global Warming Scare Real?

Few topics are discussed by President Biden more than climate change, by which he means global warming. This concern has driven many of his presidential actions, such as reducing drilling for oil in America and relying on buying foreign oil to meet our requirements. This policy has contributed to record high oil prices and has enabled Russia to finance their war in Ukraine. In turn, America has given Ukraine billions of dollars to fight against the Russian war financed by patrol dollars. I am not a climatologist and have to rely on those who are.

Aside from reading several short books on the topic, seventeen years after I first saw it, I watched again the excellent 2006 film by Al Gore, *An Inconvenient Truth.* Although I was very impressed with it in 2006 when I first saw it, I realize that seventeen years later most of his major predictions have not come to pass.

Founded in 2019, the coalition of 1,688 experts, including two Nobel laureate physicists, John Francis Clauser and Ivan Giaever, has recently published their conclusions. First, they concluded that Earth's climate has experienced several cold and warm phases since the Earth was created. The last Little Ice Age only ended in 1850, and, as we come out of the Little Ice Age, the Earth has warmed slightly. Specifically, it has warmed about 1.7 degrees Fahrenheit (equal to 1 degree Celsius) since 1880. The coalition consensus has concluded that global warming is happening, but "far slower" than predicted by the Intergovernmental Panel on Climate Change. They also concluded that "there is no climate emergency."

The validity of a climate model depends on what the model makers put into their model. Existing climate models are imperfect because not all of the many factors affecting climate are known. The coalition has concluded that existing models tend to exaggerate the effect of greenhouse gases. They ignore the fact that enriching the atmosphere with carbon dioxide (CO_2) is actually very beneficial because CO_2 is essential for all life on Earth, and extra CO_2 encourages the growth of the global plant biomass and boosts worldwide crop yields. Furthermore, a large amount of sunlight is reflected back into space by cumulus clouds, which on average, cover over half of the Earth. Therefore, for these and other reasons these models are problematic for making policy.

The coalition also rejected the claim that global warming is linked to increased natural disasters, such as hurricanes, floods, and droughts, because no compelling statistical evidence exists to support these claims. They concluded that climate science has degenerated into a discussion based on beliefs, not sound, self-critical science. Nobel laureate Francis Clauser concluded,

> The popular narrative about climate change reflects a dangerous corruption
> of science that threatens the world's economy and the well-being of billions

of people. Misguided climate science has metastasized into massive shock-journalistic pseudoscience. In turn, the [climate] pseudoscience has become a scapegoat for a wide variety of other unrelated ills.

This declaration against the climate change narrative counters propaganda spread by climate alarmists who have long predicted doomsday scenarios triggered by global warming—none of which have ever come true. Distinguished professor of Atmospheric Science and Director of the Earth System Science Center at The University of Alabama in Huntsville, John R. Christy, noted the American Western states have experienced its largest number of hot summer records in the past century, but the Ohio Valley and Upper Midwest are experiencing their fewest. For the United States as a whole, the last decade has produced an average number of records. Furthermore, the 1930s still hold the most records of extreme temperature fluctuations. Democrat presidential candidate Robert F. Kennedy Jr. even opined that climate change "is being used to control us through fear. More people are dying of bad climate change policies than they are of actual climate change." The 1,688 coalition experts agree.

September 27, 2023. Endless Immigration

My son met his wife, Alejandra (Sandra), at the University of Toronto where they were both graduate students. Sandra was Hispanic and her father was an English teacher. My son was there on a full scholarship, as she was. Soon the romance blossomed, and they married on January 10, 1998, at the Roman Catholic Transfiguration Church in New York City (she was Catholic). After they married, the immigration officer implied she married my son to get into this country, and it would not work. Obviously, this was not their intention as the marriage has lasted twenty-five years.

My son was born in Detroit; Sandra, in Logrono, in the La Rioja province of the Basque Country of Northern Spain. They both wanted to live in the United States. Then the nightmare began. They could not apply for immigration in America so had to fly to some other country, stay in a motel, then apply. Once they showed up at the immigration center at 8:00 AM and waited and waited for most of the day. At 5:00 PM they were told they would have to leave and make another appointment, so they left and made another appointment, costing them several hundred dollars. After several years of this hassle, they gave up and both my son and my daughter in-law obtained positions as professors at a University in Oslo, Norway, where they taught for six years. My son had no problems living and working in Europe. As the spouse of Sandra, my son could work in any country that was part of the European Union, which was almost every European nation. Six years later, and an offer to teach at the University of Washington, they were finally able to immigrate to the United States where they have lived ever since.

I often read about the multimillions of illegal immigrants that flow through the US southern border each year. The total immigrant population in America hit a record of 46.2 million in November 2021, the highest number ever recorded in American history going back to 1850. The number of immigrants in the country grew by over 1.5 million between November 2020 and November 2023 alone. Hispanic immigrants accounted for 924 thousand or 61 percent of the growth since last November.

A Hispanic acquaintance of mine earned her master's degree in some very technical field but could not work here in spite of the high demand for her skill. Without a work permit the many millions of illegal immigrants cannot legally work here, so live off the government for who knows how long. They are given free room and board, plus free food and medical care, plus free education for their children, and even pocket money. They even get free transportation from border areas to places where they can find a place to live. I have to wonder why so much has changed in the last decade since my daughter-in-law married my son.

For most of the immigrants, we have no knowledge of their health status, their criminal background, their education, or other relevant information. We do know that they smuggle literally tons of illegal drugs, including fentanyl, into the United States. For the last twelve months ending December 2021, the CDC projects 107 thousand to 109 thousand drug-induced deaths occurred, up by 16 percent from the previous year. Over seventy-two thousand (66 percent) of these deaths involved fentanyl and other mostly illicit synthetic opioids, often in combination with other drugs. Other problems include sex trafficking as well as exploiting children. The flow of illegals has recently increased since the government has removed large sections of the wall, allowing many more persons to walk across our paper border. Many wonder why our borders are now largely open to anyone that wants to get lots of free stuff and services. No wonder there are so many people crossing the border each and every day to come to America! And in the end, it will cost taxpayers an estimated $1trillion. I just returned from a book-speaking tour in Indianapolis, and my host paid my hotel bill. A family also staying in the motel that did not speak English had all of their expenses paid by the government. I would very much like the government to have paid for my five-day stay in the motel instead of my supporter.

October 4, 2023. Flying to Fiji

One of the advantages of being an author, whose writings are in thirteen languages, is I am frequently asked to speak in churches and colleges around the world. I have, so far, spoken in Europe, Africa, and Asia. It's hard to turn down trips that are financed by my sponsors.

I have been to Fiji twice and was recently invited again. On my first trip I flew to Los Angeles, then boarded for the twelve-hour, all-night flight to Fiji in cramped, uncomfortable seats.

When I arrived, I had to go through immigration where I was asked a dozen questions including how long I was going to stay, where I was going to stay, how much money I had with me, and what was my business there. I answered the questions that I could and later learned that, to get into the country I needed the names of people where I was going to stay. For most of the questions I admitted I did not know. I stated I was a guest of the Education Department and beyond that I had little information. The immigration officer walked away, made a few phone calls, and walked back to his interrogation station, smiled, and said to me, "Welcome to Fiji. Enjoy your stay." With that I left and caught my ride waiting for me at the airport.

The first school we visited had over nine hundred girls. As we were setting up our equipment, the girls spontaneously burst into song, mostly Christian songs. I was absolutely amazed. They sounded heavenly, all singing in perfect harmony.

All of the schools in Fiji were religious; most were openly Christian, Muslim, or Hindu. We were welcomed at all of them. I soon learned that the government was very concerned about Fiji going the way of the United States with rampant crime, tens of thousands dying from drugs such as fentanyl each year, millions of people living on the streets, and, especially, the problem we have of multimillions of illegal immigrants entering the country each year. As an island, the main entry into Fiji is through the air. I now understood the reason for the interrogation I experienced.

War and cannibalism was once everywhere. During the nineteenth century, Fijian chief Ratu Udre consumed 872 people for which he made a pile of stones to record his achievement. Ceremonial occasions saw freshly killed corpses piled up for eating. The wooden posts supporting the chief's temple had sacrificed bodies buried underneath for support. The rationale was the spirit of sacrificed persons invoked the gods to help support the structure. More men were sacrificed whenever posts had to be replaced.

Then the Christians came. The Methodist missionaries in Fiji changed the island. Rev. Thomas Baker (1832–1867) was the only missionary to be killed and eaten, along with seven of his Fijian followers. Baker's death was the basis of Jack

London's story, "The Whale Tooth." English Methodist missionary and ethnographer George Brown (1835–1917) built churches, mission houses, and schools to educate children, including Samoa Theological College.

Fiji has one of the most developed economies in the Pacific, but poor compared to our standards. They have an abundance of forest, mineral, and fish resources. The tourist industry and sugar exports are major sources of the island's income.

I spoke and distributed creation books to almost nineteen thousand students in twenty-five public high schools. We also visited the Fijian president, Jioji Konrote, for a two-hour lunch and much conversation. He explained they dealt with their endless wars and cannibalistic past by converting to Christianity and the Muslim faiths, and their goal was to maintain this tradition. He added evolutionism was especially a concern because a main reason for the loss of Christianity in the West was due to evolutionism. Before Darwin, almost all of the people of the West were theists. After Darwin, a large percentage of the population became evolutionary humanists and atheists.

While with the president, I was asked about my visit to Fiji. I mentioned it was all positive, *after* my cramped seat ride in the plane with very little leg room. On the way home, when boarding the plane, the officer asked, "Are you Jerry Bergman?" I answered, "Yes," and was asked to step aside. I wondered, "What is going on? Am I stuck here?" In ten minutes, I was told we have a new seat for you. I was given the best seat in the front of the plane that allowed me to lay back and sleep. I slept all the way home and did not awake until we landed in Los Angeles.

Me with the president of Fij

October 11, 2023. Exercise for Life

Partly to spend more time with my wife, I started attending chair yoga classes in Montpelier. After my first visit, it was apparent that the classes consisted of stretching exercises to loosen up the body's tendons and ligaments, as well as build muscle and practice deep breathing, which is helpful to supply the needed oxygen to the entire body. From my experience working as a therapist at the Toledo pain clinic, these exercises have proved very helpful to deal with neck and back pain. One of my concerns is balance, an issue I found others my age also struggle with.

In the past, I had severe back pain and sciatica for which I spent much time and money for chiropractic care, pain medicine, and even shots in my spine. Nothing helped. From reading, I learned that one common lifetime solution was certain exercises, which I have been faithfully doing for the past twenty-three years. I now rarely have back pain. At the most, I may take one Celebrex a month. From this experience, I am convinced of the efficacy of exercise. *Use it or lose it.* Doing exercise in a group ensures they are faithfully done and done right. Also, three dollars a class is cheaper than the medical clinic's physical therapy program which may cost eighty dollars an hour, although the medical clinic's physical therapy program does have the advantage of individual care.

When I was in my third year of high school, I took up weightlifting. I faithfully lifted three times a week for well over two years. I had two reasons for lifting. I was around five feet ten inches tall, 150 pounds thin, and felt looking stronger would deter being picked on and would also impress the girls. After over a year, it was apparent that I was not going to look much different in spite of my almost three hours of hard work each week. But I was much stronger. I could press close to two hundred pounds and do sit-ups with over sixty pounds held to the back of my neck with ease. Weight lifting was a great deal of work, and I moved on to other things like college, so my large double set of weights sat unused until I gave them to a friend a few years later. About ten years ago I took up weightlifting again for cardiovascular reasons, an activity that, according to my cardiologist, has done wonders for my health.

I also am an active runner, which my cardiologist also praised with an excellent report. In high school, when preparing to run a mile for track in gym class, we were told to go easy at first to save energy to finish. I knew that I was a good runner, though, so for our class exercise I took off as fast as I could. As I ran the third time around the quarter mile long track, I looked around and noticed that no one was near me. Wondering where everyone was, I looked behind me and saw the entire gym class trailing me! So, I kept up my pace. Even though I was not in training, I finished well ahead of everyone else. When I completed the run, I slowed down, as we were told to do, and a dozen or more of my fellow classmates yelled, "Way to go

Bergman! Great job!" This was the first time—ever—that I earned praise for my limited athletic ability.

Praise from peers can do wonders. To this day I endeavor to run in my daily activities, even if it was only from the parking lot to the store door. I have a dog for which a motivation to have him was to walk and, often run, to keep up with him four times a day.

I have seen so many friends my age or younger with major health problems, especially cardiovascular. They retire, spend their day watching YouTube, and gain seventy or more pounds until I no longer recognize them. No wonder in the past few years I have seen several lifelong friends pass away. The negative for my health is I am responsible for, on average, three publishable articles a week, and I had six books I authored come out this year alone. To accomplish this requires much time on the computer, writing and researching. Not good for my back, so I increased my physical activities to, I hope, compensate. Our body was designed to be engaged in an active lifestyle. *Use or lose it!*

The dog that forces me to walk

October 18, 2023. It Is Wise to Support LifeWise

Articles about the decline in attendance and influence of Christianity in America has been widely reported by the press. A March 23, 2021, headline in *The Bryan Times* reported that less than half of Americans are now members of a house of worship. One organization attempting to do something about the problem and has managed to produce very positive results is LifeWise Academy. The program was launched in 2019 by Joel Penton in Van Wert, Ohio. The program uses release-time-from-school system that requires students to be bussed to a different location off school grounds for the instruction. For Montpelier, the class location is the nearby Church of the Nazarene located on the same street as the Montpelier school. The release program has been approved by the courts and, so far, has received glowing reports. Many communities in this area have enrolled over 60 percent of eligible students. The class, which ranges in size from fifteen to twenty-five students, meets once a week for about one hour. It is staffed with several teachers to maintain proper discipline and order.

Openly religious instruction was at one time central to public education. This education helped students in their moral development and gave them a set of community wide values. The Bible and the Bible-based McGuffey Readers were once standard textbooks used in public schools for decades. The government focus was on Protestant education, so the Catholic Church started its own schools as also did the Jews. Then, in the 1950s, court rulings slowly forced public schools to become more secular. Soon they became totally secular and nonreligious, if not antireligious. Academic performance standards in many schools dropped, and misbehavior increased, as did truancy and vandalism. These problems were far less in Catholic and Hebrew schools, and the academic achievement in these schools often was superior to the public schools. For this reason, many non-Catholic parents who could afford the tuition sent their children to Catholic schools. Many educators and others realized that removing religious education resulted in many negative consequences. Reasons for the decline of quality education in public schools include they lost education's fundamental purpose of producing well-rounded students who succeeded in their work, family, and life.

Enter LifeWise that produced a program which focuses, not only on academic achievement, but also character development, mental and social health, and community involvement. The LifeWise program covers knowing what the Bible teaches and learning about God and His will for us, ourselves, and our world. The program covers the human heart and soul, examining how the Bible accounts tie into, and point to, the big picture of creation. The last goal is to explore ways students can live out the changed character that the program stresses.

The lessons begin with Genesis, helping students to understand that in the beginning God created everything, the Earth, the universe, and all life. God made all of creation including light, land, sky, stars, planets, and all of the plants and animals. God then pronounced His creation very good. Creation was perfect, as God intended, until the fall. The LifeWise five-year program covers all sixty-six books of the Bible ending with the Book of Revelation.

I am not aware how carefully the creation/evolution issue will be covered. I do know the research that determined thousands of persons who knew the scriptures and had some knowledge of the science against Darwinism did not survive the evolutionary indoctrination common in high schools and colleges today. Especially, introductory biology classes, the classes that I taught, are very heavy on the claimed evidence for evolution, including the fossil record, vestigial organs, homology, ontology recapitulates phylogeny, junk DNA, biogeography, and anatomical similarities among living organisms, including DNA and embryos. Students need to be able to respond to these claims with facts.

Regardless, the results of research show a reverse correlation between religious measures and deviance, drug abuse, and alcohol abuse and a positive relationship (a direct correlation) with mental health, life satisfaction, a more positive self-perception, and greater academic achievement. In the end, LifeWise may help to change our community.

A country school house around 1900

October 25, 2023. Adam and Astronomy: Fully Complete Creations

One of the most controversial areas of the creation worldview is the short time during which the Bible teaches that the creation took place. Actually, this view is very logical. The creation of Adam could not have involved much time because he must have been created as a fully functioning human with blood traversing in his circulatory system to be alive. Lack of blood to his brain for five minutes would have ended his life. A person becomes unconscious during cardiac arrest within twenty seconds after the heart stops beating. Without the oxygen and the sugars it needs to function, the brain is unable to deliver the electrical signals needed to maintain breathing and organ function. After only three minutes, global cerebral ischemia—the lack of blood flow to the entire brain—leads to brain injury that becomes progressively worse after each second. To create a lung, heart, and his other organs *separately* would not work. Without the protection of the body, and its nutrient circulation, these organs would rapidly deteriorate. Consequently, Adam would have to be created *ex nihilo* with a fully functioning body and oxygenated blood traversing through his body.

If our newly created Adam could be examined by a modern doctor, he would conclude that Adam was a very healthy mature twenty-five-year-old (or so) man, even though he was actually only a few hours old. Adam thus had the "appearance of age." Conversely, he would not have any of the negative signs of aging, such as the beginnings of plaque in his arteries and veins. Arterial plaque occurs when cholesterol builds up in the arteries' inner linings. Nor would he have the normal cellular deterioration which slowly builds up and is not normally apparent until we are in our forties.

The same is true of the solar system. It must exist as a complete operational unit to function. One example is the moon's critical role is required for life to exist on the Earth's surface. The origin of our moon has dumbfounded cosmologists for over a century and still does. One popular theory was the Capture Theory. As the moon was orbiting around the sun with the Earth, it was captured by the Earth's gravitational field. Aside from the improbability of this event, the question of where the moon came from is still a mystery. Compared to all other moons, our moon is enormous in relation to the size of the Earth. Trips to the Moon by creationist James Irwin allowed moon rock to be brought back, which created problems for the Capture Theory. The moon rocks were far too much like the Earth to have come from some distant part of the solar system.

A few of the other origin of the moon theories include the Fission Theory, the Condensation Theory, and the Giant Impact Theory. According to the Giant Impact

Theory, at some point in Earth's very early history, the moon formed as a result of a massive collision between the Earth and a planet about the size of Mars. The debris from this impact collected in an orbit around Earth to eventually coalesce to form the moon. The problem with this theory is, where did the Mars-sized planet come from? The theory assumes before Earth and the moon existed, a proto-Earth and a smaller planet called Theia existed. The problem is that absolutely no valid evidence exists for the Giant Impact Theory except for it being superior to the other competing theories since it can explain why the moon's rocks are so similar to the Earth's.

Our solar system's planets are all held in their orbit in a smooth-running system by our giant sun's gravity. To produce the required stable solar system, God could not have created a bunch of planets that are moving everywhere willy-nilly. As a bike is stable when moving, but will fall over when not moving, likewise the planets are stable only when moving. This is a requirement for life to exist on our planet.

The Earth not only spins on its axis at 24,898 mph but orbits the sun at an average speed of 67,000 mph, or 18.5 miles per second. The entire solar system is moving at an average speed of 448,000 mph (720,000 km/h). At this rate it would take about 230 million years to travel all the way around the Milky Way Galaxy, which is where our solar system is located. The Milky Way Galaxy itself is moving at a speed of twenty-five miles per second. Our galaxy is part of the *Local Group* of galaxies that, as a group, are moving at the truly astonishing rate of 375 miles per second toward the Virgo Supercluster. The Virgo Supercluster is an enormous collection of galaxies some forty-five million light-years away from Earth. In short, the entire universe must exist as a functional unit, just like the human body. Its movement produces the stability that we experience on Earth. Of the over five thousand confirmed exoplanets out of the billions of stars in our galaxy, none show any evidence of life. It appears that the entire universe was created as a functional unit for humans, just as our body was also created as a functional unit.

These enormous distances are a major reason why scientists believe the universe is old. New discoveries by the James Webb telescope found a remarkable assemblage of five thousand not *relatively young* galaxies as evolutionists expected but galaxies that looked about as old as the galaxies near our Earth, providing evidence that the entire universe was created about the same time. Among them, one galaxy, the youngest to date, unveiled an array of extraordinary cosmic phenomena to the point that scientists are baffled as to how it is even possible. The problem is: at the edge of the universe, we expect to find young galaxies. When viewing a galaxy that a is few billion light years away, we are seeing what it looked like a few billion years ago. The problem is a lot of what we are seeing has proven very hard for scientists to understand.

Picture of the Earth taken from the moon

November 1, 2023. The Secular Creation Story

Some people, given the enormity in size and distance of our universe, question how the Genesis creation account could be true. Consequently, let us look at the other side, the secular story, of the creation of the universe. I have an interest in this area because I taught astronomy at the college level and what follows is what we taught. Eminent cosmologist, the late Cambridge University Professor Steven Hawking is "one of the most celebrated and respected personalities of our century…, the Einstein of our time." He spent the last two decades of his life attempting to produce a rational explanation for his naturalistic origin of the universe belief. The main problem he had to overcome is, in his words, "The universe is so well suited to life that it can appear to be designed." Evolutionists believe it was *not* designed, though, but rather it evolved, so they need to explain the origin of a universe that looks like it was designed but was not.

Both the evolutionists and creationists agree that in the beginning there was nothing, no matter, energy, space, or time. Evolutionists teach that the universe began with an infinitely hot and dense single point called a "singularity" smaller than a molecule. This singularity exploded at unimaginable speeds over the next 13.7 billion years to produce the cosmos existing today. How nothing produced the singularity and where it came from and why it banged is unknown.

Hawking believed that, just as life had evolved, similarly the universe evolved by a process akin to how life on Earth evolved. What caused the Big Bang's evolution that produced our Earth is unknown. In short, this Big Bang scenario has created far more questions than it solves. If the universe follows the laws of physics, it is, therefore, largely independent of how we conceptualize the universe.

Hawking explains that religion was the only answer to the question where matter and life came from until modern science began developing about two hundred years ago. Now, he informs us, science has shown that the religion side is wrong. In Hawking's words, "Science provides better and more consistent answers, but people will always cling to religion, because it gives comfort, and they do not…understand science." Hawking, in his newest book, explains how life was created without God as follows:

> Somehow, some…atoms came to be arranged in the form of molecules of DNA…. As DNA reproduced itself, there would have been random errors, many of which would have been harmful, and…a few errors would have been favorable to the survival of the species—these would have been chosen by Darwinian natural selection.

Thus, he concludes, humans, and all life, are the result of chance mutations causing billions of mistakes. The science of genetics has documented that 99.9 percent of such mutation mistakes are ultimately harmful. Furthermore, they add up to eventually produce genetic meltdown of the organism, causing cancer or other diseases, and death, *not* progressive evolution.

Hawking has proceeded with his creative musings specifically to support his preconceived conclusion, namely, to bolster his belief that the universe created itself out of nothing. This violates the Law of Causality, that for every event there must exist a sufficient cause. In contrast to this approach, he should determine *from the evidence* which view is correct, creative design or evolutionary chance. According to the Bible, the Earth was designed for life (Ps. 115:16; Isa. 45:18) and the universe was created specifically to support that role.

This Big Bang cosmology is widely taught in schools and books. One typical example is a book published for children titled *Why? Over 1,111 Answers to Everything.* In answer to the question "What is the Big Bang" the book's answer is: "The 'big bang' is the name for the leading theory behind the birth of everything: atoms, light, gravity, gasses, stars, planets, galaxies and even time itself. And…scientists have found plenty of evidence to back up the big bang theory [page 82]." The text adds that, before the big bang "nothing, nada, zip" existed [page 83]. The article then dogmatically outlines the scenario mentioned above without ever so much as hinting about the many problems with the big bang. Students reading this, and many other references including their textbooks, will conclude that the big bang is proven fact based on evidence, which is not the case. Nor will they hear the other side in public schools because the American courts have ruled that only one side, the nontheistic side, can be taught in public schools. My short introductory paragraphs above would not be allowed.

The Late Professor Steven Hawking

November 8, 2023. A Chance Meeting Changes a Life

One topic often asked when a married couple is introduced is "How did you two meet?" One of the most interesting introductions I have ever heard was told by the husband. This is his story.

How did we meet? I was slowly jogging toward the auditorium door of the building I was in and saw what looked like a young Mexican girl. The Mexican girl held her hand out from her body, her palm pointing in my direction. I held up my hand near hers, and as I moved next to her our hands met, we both tightened our grip, and I spun around facing the direction I just came from. We then both started walking together hand in hand, and she asked me, "Where are we going?" I answered, "Wherever you want to go." She was sixteen and I was seventeen, a senior in high school a few weeks from graduation. We have now been together for over a half century.

My father was missing in action and likely died in the Korean War. My mother spent the rest of her life grieving. She was a good mother and took very good care of me. Mother was just not a very happy person to be around. I do not ever remember her giving me a hug or saying a kind word about me or anything that I did. As an only child I felt something was missing in my life. When I met Angelina that day, we sat down together and talked, engaging in some introductions, including our names, where we lived, and why we were at the musical program. She told me her father was a preacher and her mom and dad lived in Detroit near Six Mile Road. She was with her Black girlfriend, Gabrielle, who was older than Angelina and out of school.

After Gabrielle caught up with us, she offered to take both of us home. I thanked her and mentioned that it would not work out because my car was parked outside. So, Gabrielle suggested I take Angelina home. She did not know that we just met that day and assumed we were good friends. So, I drove Angelina home from the music festival.

I was at the music festival trying out for a small part. My passion was music. I was close to being accepted for a part in a musical play, so I was in a good mood that day. I had always wanted to be a singer, so thought I would try out.

Angelina's home was in a solid middle-class neighborhood. She opened the door, and we walked in. "Mom and Dad," she said with a smile, "I would like you to meet someone. This is David, a friend." Her father, an African American, looked like a football player, which he was in high school. Her mother was a petite energetic German. I liked them immediately. Their warm smile and engaging personality shined.

After an hour of visiting, Angelina invited me to her father's church. I hesitated, but as this would enable me to spend more time with her, I accepted. I was not a church-going guy. My mother insisted I go every Sunday. It was boring. The sermon groaned on and was even worse than school. We had communion about every week, or so it seemed. "This is My body," the pastor said, lifting up the bread. It did not look like a body to me. It looked like a stale piece of bread. "This is My blood," the pastor said, lifting up the glass of wine. It did not look like blood to me, thankfully. It looked like a glass of grape juice. I thought, what a waste of time.

The following Sunday, I was at Angelina's father's church. I was greeted with smiles and amens and felt at home and warm in the all-Black congregation he pastored. The church choir was incredible. I found what I was missing at home. My life was music, then and now, and I fell in love with this congregation. Angelina's father gave a dynamic sermon on forgiveness. I walked away telling myself I really learned something! When they asked about why I was at the auditorium where I met Angelina, they learned about my love of music. I was in the center front of the choir the next week. The congregation saw themselves like a dark chocolate cake and me as icing on the cake. So, from that day on, I was not David, but Icing.

I married Angelina and her father performed the wedding. I ended up in seminary earning a BA in Music and Music Ministry. My mother was surprised that someone who hated church is now a music minister in a large Calvary Chapel church. I think she was both proud and, for the first time since she lost my father, genuinely happy. She even joined our church, met a guy there, and remarried.

One horrible event was we lost our firstborn who was riding his tricycle down our sloped driveway. The three-year-old ended up in the street, killed by a car. The driver, we found out later, was drunk. Angelina's father made it clear that this tragedy, which should bring a couple together, often does the opposite, resulting in a divorce. We consciously kept our lip buttoned about it, and our marriage, as Angelina's father promised, became stronger. Thank God for the music festival where we met.

November 15, 2023. Israel Attacked—College Students Applaud

On October 7, 2023, Israel was the victim of one of the most horrific terrorist attacks in modern history. The heavily armed Hamas gunmen drove into civilian areas slaughtering everyone within reach, including women and children, Israelites and Americans. Over 1,800 Israelis were killed, thousands injured, and hundreds were taken hostage. Cell phones recorded in real time some of the worst atrocities of the modern era: beheadings, raping women, burning children in front of their parents, and parents in front of their children. At one Israeli community, close to 80 percent of the 280 murdered victims, including children, bore signs of torture. Israel rapidly responded to stop the slaughter, launching numerous airstrikes into Hamas-controlled Gaza in what is likely to be a long and brutal war.

Hamas was founded in 1987 specifically to annihilate Israel and the Jewish people. This goal was written into their charter. In 1987, the first intifada (Palestinian uprising), 160 Jews and over one thousand Palestinians were killed. Since 1987 Hamas has been responsible for hundreds of suicide bombings and deadly attacks on Israeli civilians. The US State Department formally designated Hamas a terrorist group in 1997. In a 2005 land-for-peace deal Israel forced nine thousand Jews from the Gaza Strip to give Muslims total control of the area. The land-for-peace deal soon failed. Hamas won the 2006 Gaza parliamentary elections, and in 2007 violently seized control of the Gaza Strip from the internationally recognized Palestinian Authority. In the 2000–2005 intifada, over another one thousand Jews and three thousand Palestinians were killed.

Soon after the latest October 2023 intifada, massive protests broke out in America, not against the group causing the atrocities, *but against the victims of the atrocities, the Israelis.* Students at Harvard, Columbia, George Washington, and scores of other colleges and universities witnessed large numbers of anti-Israel protesters. They demanded a cease fire, meaning Israel should do nothing to stop the thousands of rockets that are killing thousands of Jews as I write this.

When the current American administration came into office, they drastically cut US oil production, causing the world price to drastically increase. The result was Iran's oil profits rose by billions of dollars, much of which, instead of using it for humanitarian purposes, was given to Hamas to purchase the tens of thousands of the rockets they used to attack Israel. Added to this were the billions of dollars the Biden administration allocated to Iran, which ended up supporting Hamas's attacks against Israel.

ISRAEL'S FOUNDING

In 1516, the Ottoman Turks invaded and occupied Palestine until 1918 when Britain occupied the country. After World War II, having few choices and fleeing persecution in Europe and Arab countries, millions of Jews moved into the area where Jews have lived for the past two thousand years. Instead of the Palestinians assimilating these refugees, as was done with other groups, Jews faced continued persecution as they have in most countries for most of modern history. If a million highly trained Muslim Arabs instead of Jews immigrated to Palestine, they would have been welcomed, documenting the fact that the main issue in the current war is anti-Semitism. To solve the Israel/Arab conflict, two states were formed from the former Palestine by the United Nations in 1947, and Israel became independent in May 1948. Islam is now the second-largest religion in Israel, constituting 1.707 million persons or 18 percent of the country's population. Ethnic Arab citizens make up the majority of Muslims in Israel. In the war against Israel, thousands of Muslims are also being killed. So fanatical is Hamas that they want the Jews to perish even if thousands of Arab Muslims also die.

Israel's counteroffensive in Gaza has, since October 7, 2023, according to the Palestinian Health Ministry, killed over 10,515 people, over half under age eighteen. Authorities estimate that the final death toll will be over half a million Gaza residents, and several thousand young Israelis will die. One estimate is that over thirty-seven thousand pregnant women will be forced to give birth with no electricity or proper medical supplies in Gaza in the coming months, risking life-threatening complications for themselves and their babies. If the estimated $50 billion Hamas spent for war was used to help the Gaza people, their lives would have vastly improved. In the end, the enormous carnage and suffering of both Israelis and Gaza people is due to anti-Semitic hate. To Hamas, if they can snuff out the life of thousands of Jews, their loss is well worth it.

One fact is clear. Many of the student protestors, in siding with the brutal terrorists, have very little knowledge of the problem. One sign read: "When people are occupied, resistance is justified." I could add, "except if the occupiers are Turks." Another protestor said, "We must finish the work of Hitler and exterminate all Jews." In calling Jews' attempts to defend themselves genocide, protestors are either ignorant of, or have chosen to ignore, the facts. The behavior of anti-Semites at elite universities includes threats to harm Jewish students. This is yet another reason why more parents and students are thinking twice about the value and wisdom of a college education, not to mention the often six-digit cost of attending a university.

November 22, 2023. Meeting a Holocaust Survivor

When in high school, I sometimes passed out Christian tracts to householders. Most people politely said "No, thanks," so I moved on to the next house. Only one encounter stands out. In the wealthy community of Bloomfield Hills, Michigan, I knocked on the door of a mansion. An elderly man opened the door, stepped outside with me, and closed the door. Judging by his accent, he was obviously from Germany. After my surprise abated, I rapidly realized I had never before encountered a person with such obvious anger when passing out tracts. He did not tell me his name, so I will call him Wilhelm. I knew his anger was not against me (I just met him), so I just listened to him. I felt he needed someone to talk to, and I was curious about him. As I was standing on his porch listening to him, I noticed a luxury car in his driveway; I was from Detroit, so I often noticed cars. Wilhelm explained his father was a Jew but was not considered a Jew in Nazi Germany because according to the Nuremberg Laws, only a person with three or four Jewish grandparents was a Jew, and Wilhelm only had two.

Wilhelm's father, a Lutheran minister, was a mischling (German for "mixling") because he had three Jewish grandparents. He explained the Lutheran church expelled all ethnic Jewish ministers even though they converted to Christianity, some when they were quite young. Wilhelm's father not only converted but became an ordained Lutheran minister. Jews who converted to Christianity, including Wilhelm's father, were usually sent to a concentration camp. Mischlinge (plural for "mischling") was a pejorative legal term used in Nazi Germany to denote persons of a mixed "Aryan" and non-Aryan race. The Nazis enacted the Nuremberg Laws to apply the belief widely held by scientists then about inferior races into law. They believed that the world is divided into distinct races that are not equally strong and valuable. The Nazis considered Germans to be members of the superior "Aryan" race, the strongest, and most valuable race. Intermarriage, they believed, "polluted" the pure race.

Although Nazi Germany was an overwhelmingly Christian nation, predominately Lutheran, with similarly overwhelmingly self-identified Christian leadership, it did very little to oppose Nazism. They also did little to help Wilhelm's father and, by expelling him from the church, exposed him to the Nazis. As a result, he was imprisoned and died in a prison camp after being worked to death. If he was allowed to continue leading his church, he may well have stayed in the shadows. The church did not want to get involved in politics but stuck to preaching the gospel and allowed the secular state to run the country.

Wilhelm lost his Jewish father but nonetheless was not enough Jewish to be sent to the camps, so was drafted into the Nazi army where he served honorably. The story Wilhelm patiently explained to me illustrated the fact that his wealth could not compensate for his loss. After close to thirty years, he was still very bitter about what happened to his devout Christian Lutheran minister father who happened to have one to many Jewish grandfathers. I have no idea how he became wealthy and did not ask. I just listened to his story. He needed someone to ventilate to, and I was glad to help him in some small way by serving as a good listener. After he thanked me and explained his family was tired of listening to his past, I left and never forgot his story. My encounter was like, when flying, persons sitting next to you may tell you intimate details about their life, that they would never tell friends, because they know they will probably never see you again.

November 29, 2023. A Harvard-Trained Professor Expelled

In the past, tenure was generally an effective protection against termination based on one's conclusions about Darwinism. But *not any longer*. Professor Change Laura Tan, a tenured associate professor of molecular biology at the University of Missouri, was terminated due to her rejection of Darwinism. Her PhD was from the University of Pennsylvania in biochemistry, and she did a genetics postdoctoral fellowship at Harvard Medical School.

Dr. Tan was born and grew up in mainland China. She first learned about Darwin's theory of evolution in middle school in China. She accepted without question the idea that life came from nonlife, that humans were a type of animal that evolved from some ape ancestor, and that there is no God. Dr. Tan became a Christian in 2004 but remained an evolutionist because she believed evolution was firmly supported by science. It was only when she began to teach molecular biology at the University of Missouri that she began to question the theory.

From teaching and doing research, she learned that the genes used to accomplish DNA replication, transcription, and translation in the three domains of life, i.e., bacteria, archaea, and eukaryotes, are all very distinct. This was clear evidence that prokaryotes did not evolve into eukaryotes as evolution teaches. Furthermore, the three domains of life could not share a common ancestor, a conclusion based on the fact that *most of the essential genes are domain-of-life specific*. In other words, most of the required genes were very different, producing an impassable gap between prokaryotes and eukaryotes.

The more she studied and researched the genomes of different organisms, the more she became convinced that all organisms on Earth are better represented diagrammatically as a forest of separate phyla trees, instead of only one evolutionary tree as taught by Darwinism. She also studied *orphan genes*, genes unique to a specific species that are not found in other species. Tan documented that approximately 29.8 percent of the total protein-coding genes were orphan genes while less than 0.01 percent were universal genes (genes with homologs in each of the 317 species she analyzed). This was the exact opposite of what evolution predicted, and a stunning indictment of the theory!

PROBLEMS BEGAN

Her major problem was that her opposers found out she was publishing articles critical of evolutionary naturalism. One of her main co-authors was the head of the genetics lab at Clemson University. Her book on genetics was co-authored with Dr. Rob Stadler, a PhD in medical engineering from Harvard. The book was very well-received, earning 115 reviews on Amazon, with 90 percent three-star ratings or better, and 80 percent five stars. When the knowledge of her "heresy" was made public, her grant re-application was rejected. Her laboratory and office were moved from a modern and well-equipped building to an old and deteriorated building.

Subsequently, the then interim dean informed her that the University decided to dismiss her. At that time, she was one of the most productive associate professors, with excellent student ratings. Nonetheless, her peers disparaged any publication that took umbrage with Darwinism. The interim dean said that she could resign to avoid the dismissal process or could request a hearing. She chose the hearing with little idea about what would transpire. In addition to members of the University of Missouri Campus Tenure Faculty Committee, a court reporter, a videographer, and six lawyers were in the room. The committee had a lawyer, and her dean had three lawyers. She was there alone. The vague charges for which she was being fired claimed there was

> adequate cause for dismissal related directly and substantially to your fitness or performance in a professional capacity of teacher or researcher. … [And for failing to] perform your responsibilities in research at levels satisfactory to maintain your tenured appointment.

It was clear from the academic hearing that the root issue was her molecular biology research which documented the fact that the life-from-nonlife belief, and the evolutionary notion that eukaryotes evolved from prokaryotes, were both at odds with the experimental evidence. She presented at the meeting some of the evidence that led her to question the validity of Darwinism. No one could dispute the indisputable facts she presented. She did not accept Darwinism and that was her problem. On June 29, 2022, the Board of Curators informed her that they had decided "to sustain the decision by the Hearing Committee" to dismiss her. She has been unemployed since then and may go back to China where they are looking for highly trained Harvard-educated scientists.

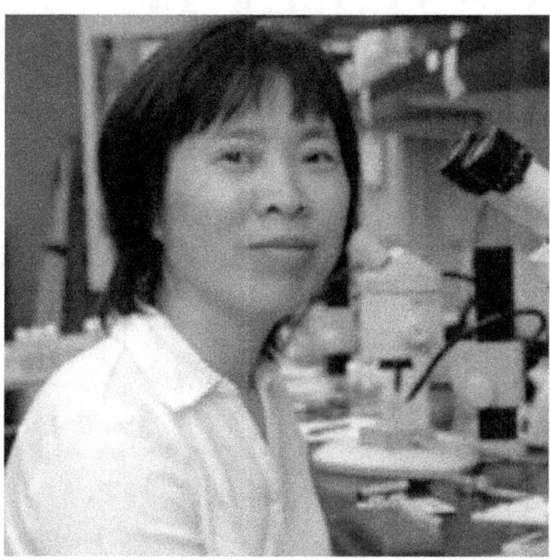

Laura Tan, PhD, Harvard-trained scientist in her lab

December 6, 2023. I'm Back in a Science Lab: Testing a Plesiosaur Vertebra Bone

On a recent trip to present a paper at the Creation Evidence Museum in Glen Rose, Texas, I had the opportunity to help prepare thin sections of a dinosaur era bone to look for evidence of the protein collagen. Bones are not solids of calcium as often assumed, but living organs that grow and repair themselves throughout the lifetime of the animal. The museum lab had access to a vertebra from a marine reptile plesiosaur (genus *Plesiosaurus*). The dinosaur was assigned by evolutionists as living in the Late Cretaceous, from 100.5 million years to 66 million years ago. The vertebra I elected to sample came from the Taylor Group in the North Sulfur River Channel of Fannin County, Texas. Collagen is a tough protein found throughout bones, making them resilient, yet flexible. Oxygen and other chemicals react with collagen, gradually breaking it down into tiny molecules. We were concerned with the age of the bone, and thus how long ago the plesiosaur lived.

The popular view of its age is illustrated by a sign for the fossil section of the Carnegie Museum of Natural History in Pittsburgh that claimed, "Fossils that are traces of prehistoric life have no original organic parts preserved." Such claims readily appear throughout popular science media, so it is no wonder that few scientists know about evidence of original organic tissues in fossils, and even fewer bother looking for the evidence.

Dr. Mary Schweitzer and her team first caught the world's attention about tissue preservation in a 2005 *Science* paper that described intact blood vessels and red blood cells in a *Tyrannosaurus rex* bone. If fossils are traces of life that lived many millions of years ago, then we have no reason to believe that complex organic molecules like collagen could be preserved, let alone cells or whole blood vessels. But many fossils *do contain* these structures. Hardly a month passes by without new reports of "soft tissue" discovered in supposedly "million-year-old" fossils. Could this organic material really be preserved for millions of years? I wanted to determine for myself the age of these fossils.

The plesiosaur vertebra bone I selected was cut and polished using a precision machine designed to obtain a thin slice. The wafer-thin slice was then examined using a fluorescent microscope. Fluorescent microscopes use high intensity light to examine the specimen which excites certain minerals, causing them to fluoresce, i.e., glow. The fluorescent minerals in turn emit a lower-energy light of a longer wavelength as do fluorescent light bulbs commonly used in offices and homes.

Fluorescence is one technique used to identify soft-tissue remains within the wavelength of 315–490 nm. By this technique we were able to detect clear evidence of collagen. The tryptophan and tyrosine within type I collagen naturally glows with strongly fluorescent properties. Collagens play an important role in the structure and function of skin, cartilage, bone, and connective tissue. Its molecular formula is $C_4H_6N_2O_3R_2 \cdot (C_7H_9N_2O_2R)_n$. My examination, which found evidence of collagen, indicates that this bone could not even be close to sixty-six million years old as assumed by evolutionists.

In this research we focused on biochemicals that have measured decay rates, like collagen and DNA. Some reports mention original hemoglobin (a blood protein) and pigments (like squid ink) in fossils claimed to be "tens-of-millions-of-years" old, but their survival times are not known with experimental certainty. Unfortunately, evolutionists look at this evidence with their "evolution glasses" and attempt to explain it away by claiming, for example, that the results are due to contamination of the bone from outside sources. This area requires more study, but it is critical that the evidence be allowed to speak for itself without viewing it through either creation or evolutionary glasses.

Me examining the plesiosaur vertebrae

In the lab with the scientists pointing out the collagen

December 13, 2023. I Was Vindicated: The Human Eye Is Not Poorly Designed

One claim that is repeatedly printed in the scientific literature is that the human eye is backward, which is worse than poor design. The reason for this claim is the light-sensing cells are in the *back* of the retina cells, requiring light to pass through layers of neurons and capillaries before it reaches the photosensitive part of the rods and cones. Evolutionists explain the wiring of the human eye as a product of our unfortunate evolutionary baggage.

Oxford University Professor Richard Dawkins wrote that the most glaring example of imperfection in the human body is the retina:

> Imagine a latter-day Helmholtz presented by an engineer with a digital camera, with its screen of tiny photocells, set up to capture images projected directly to the screen surface. But now, suppose the eye's "photocells" are pointing backwards, *away* from the scene being looked at. The "wires" connecting the photocells to the brain run over all the surface of the retina, so the light rays have to pass through a carpet of wires before they hit the photocells. That design doesn't make sense.

He added:

> One consequence of the photocells pointing backwards is that the wires which carry their data somehow have to pass through the retina and back to the brain. What they do, in the vertebrate eye, is converge on a particular hole in the retina, where they dive through it. The hole is called the blind spot, because it is blind, but…it is quite large, more like a blind patch. …Once again, send it back to the designer. It's not just bad design, it's the design of a complete idiot." (From: Richard Dawkins, *Greatest Show on Earth,* 2010, pp. 353–355)

I reasoned that, as a creationist, there must be a good reason for this design. My evolutionary colleagues exclaimed, "Face it. Evolution is right, creation is wrong. There is no way to explain this idiotic design except by evolution."

I did a lot of reading on this topic, even asking my eye doctor, Dr. Terra Richmond, for suggestions. Intrigued, she spent some time reviewing her college ophthalmology textbooks and provided much insight to the problem, but still no good answer. As I was then a graduate student at the Medical College of Ohio in Toledo, I took an independent study on the problem. The professor was intrigued with the problem as well, and together we combed the literature.

I eventually learned critical reasons for the retina's reverse design. One is the fact that it allows the rods and cones to connect with the retinal pigment epithelial cells that provide nutrients to the retina, recycle photopigments, and provide an opaque layer to absorb excessive light. The pigment epithelial cells thus connect directly with the blood supply required to maintain their life. Furthermore, the pigment epithelium tissue performs numerous other functions that are critical for retina viability and activity. One is that it phagocytizes 10 percent of the mass of each photoreceptor outer segment on a diurnal schedule and constantly restores the chromophore to the 11-cis-retinal form from its all-trans configuration, permitting visual pigment synthesis and regeneration. Still other reasons, not mentioned here, could be provided to document why this design is actually required for vision to exist. Even the blind spot that Dawkins claimed is "quite large, more like a blind patch" in fact takes up less than 1 percent of the retinal surface. We are not normally aware of it because the brain fills in the missing information which it obtains from the other eye.

I eventually published my findings in a peer-reviewed scientific journal. The article was titled, "Is the Inverted Human Eye a Poor Design?" and was published in *Journal of the American Scientific Affiliation* 52(1):18–30, March 2000. The view that the backward-retina design is required for vision is now widely accepted in the scientific community, and I would like to believe that my work made a small contribution to solving the problem. One recent article in the journal *Current Biology* on the history of the issue, gave many reasons why the vertebrate-eye design is a sterling example of excellent design. This design produced the eyes of the eagle that allow it to see a mouse two miles (3.2 kilometers) away. For comparison, a human with excellent vision may be able to see the same animal less than one city-block (0.3 kilometers) away. Ironically, the *Current Biology* article listed the human inverted eye as an example of the amazing ability of *evolution* (not God) to design things.

December 20, 2023. Banning Christmas

During my first two decades at Northwest State College, we had a Christmas party every year. All college faculty, staff, administrators, and their spouses were invited. The meals were superb, as was the conversation. It gave all of us a chance to get to know people in other departments, as well as to get to know each other better. We often talked shop, but family, children, and other interests were usually discussed as well. We also had excellent, often live, entertainment. It was an event we all looked forward to, even the atheists. Then, as I understand what happened, the lawyers got involved and somehow concluded that our Christmas party was a violation of separation of church and state. Our Christmas party was not a church but a get-together which existed since the college was founded in 1968. So ended our once-a-year get-together.

We also used to have many Christmas decorations around the college, and the lawyers, so I am told, wanted to make sure they all met the required constitutional mustard. After the evaluation, all that was left was colored Christmas tree bulbs. Most of the decorations did not pass the Constitution sniff test. The candy canes were removed because the white stands for the purity of Christ, and the red for the blood of Christ. Of course, the manger, and all figures relating to Christ's birth, were removed.

Ironically, the claim that "the Constitution requires a wall of separation between Church and State" is *not in the US Constitution*. It was in a letter that Thomas Jefferson wrote to the Baptist Congregation in Danbury, Connecticut, in 1802. Jefferson's meaning is clear when the entire letter is read. His conclusion was, "the first amendment has erected a wall of separation between Church and State. That wall is a one-dimensional wall. It keeps the government from running the Church, while making sure Christian principles will always stay in government."

As eloquently said by many others, Jefferson was referring to a conclusion long held in American government that, for most of its first three centuries the Constitution prevented the government from meddling into the church's business but, as a democracy, the church can influence the government. This is allowed for any other group, as is true of any majority-run government. The influence of the Christian majority in our government is still found everywhere from the swearing in of the president on a Bible, to the prayers that open every session of Congress, to the "In God We Trust" on our coins.

The constitutional phrase: "Congress shall make no law respecting an *establishment* of religion, or prohibiting the free exercise thereof" meant that Congress was prohibited from establishing an official state religious denomination. Eight of the thirteen British colonies originally had official, or "established," churches, and in those states dissenters who sought to practice or proselytize a different version of Christianity, were sometimes persecuted. Laws mandated that everyone attend the official state house of worship and pay taxes that funded the salaries of their ministers. Most New Englanders went to Congregationalist church services. They were held in a meeting house which served secular as well as religious functions. The meeting house was a small wood building located at the center of town.

By the eighteenth century, the vast majority of all colonists were churchgoers. Church attendance in some areas was then 70 percent of the adult local population. The New England colonists—with the exception of Rhode Island—were predominantly Puritans, who led strict religious lives. The highly educated clergy were devoted to the study and teaching of both Scripture and God's creation, i.e., the natural sciences. In 2022, an average of only 34 percent of US adults said they had attended a church, synagogue, mosque, or temple in the past seven days. Church attendance is about twice as high among Republicans as compared to Democrats. Banning Christmas is only one indicator of where our country is heading. So few people attend church that my grandkids have sports practice and tournaments on Sunday morning, and the usual Wednesday evening church service now is football practice. Welcome to secular Europe.

December 27, 2023. A Capable Wife Is Priceless and Obtains the Lord's Favor

One day this month was one of the most important days of my life. It was on a frigid snowy day of December 28, thirty-eight years ago when I married my wife, Dianne. Since then I was blessed with a wonderful relationship. Not a day goes by where I don't appreciate how fortunate I am to be married to her. As the Scriptures state, "He who finds a good, capable wife finds a priceless jewel and obtains favor from the Lord" (Prov. 18:22). And "a capable, intelligent, and virtuous woman…is far more precious than jewels and her value is far above rubies or pearls. The heart of her husband trusts in her confidently and relies on, and believes in, her securely" (Prov. 31:10–11). As Proverbs 31:16 explains: "She gives careful thought to a field and then buys it. She then plants a thriving grape-vine garden from the money she has earned." According to the Scriptures, my talented businesswoman wife Dianne is perfect.

All marriages involve compromise, mine included. We came from different worlds. I was born in Detroit and grew up in a Detroit suburb. Dianne was born in northwest Ohio and spent almost her entire life in Montpelier. We also had more than our fair share of challenges. When God created Eve from Adam's side, He stated that Eve was created to be a complement of Adam, not a twin or a clone, but a new creation, different in many ways than a man. Some things I learned in college have helped me negotiate these differences in married life.

When we married, I was still teaching at the University of Toledo. As a result, I was gone a lot, which put the responsibility on her for dealing with the four children in our new blended family. This was a very difficult time for her, but she dealt with it. And I admire her greatly for sticking with it. When the kids went off to college, it allowed us some time for ourselves. I have always traveled a lot, speaking at churches and testifying as an expert witness in courts around the country based on the books, articles, and law review articles that I have written.

When I get upset at something, she settles me down, usually successfully. When she gets upset, I do likewise. A good rule is never let disagreements carry into the evening. Attempt to agree on a compromise and move forward. One rule I was careful to follow which often helps couples with the inevitable conflicts in marriage is this. Never, ever put your spouse down, especially in front of others. Demeaning your spouse demeans you. If you call her stupid, what does that say about you? You married her.

I have had to swallow my pride more than once and admit Dianne is more often right then wrong. One issue we must deal with is I am color blind. One result is Dianne is sometimes embarrassed at times to let me out of the house wearing some weird color combinations. When I travel on speaking tours, she selects my clothing combinations so as to not to embarrass me or her. Marriage survival requires each spouse to realize, and accommodate for, their differences. When I am sure my decision is the best one and Dianne disagrees, I have to think: "My male friends may agree with me, but my wife is not a man. She is a woman and sees the world through a woman's eyes."

We now enjoy spending time, often on the phone or texting, with our four grown children and their four spouses. Most are college-educated and have done very well in their careers and with their family. We also have ten grandchildren, eight girls and two boys. Unfortunately, as is often true today, none of our children live in the Montpelier area, but all over the country. My son and daughter-in-law have lived in Europe for over a decade. And my daughter and her husband lived in Houma, Louisiana, for close to twenty years. In our modern world, career is often first, and, as a result, family often suffers, but we attempt to deal with this fact as best we can. Especially now, in our retirement, we enjoy spending time with each other shopping and taking care of tasks around the house.